Ending Book Hunger

Ending Book Hunger

Access to Print Across Barriers of Class and Culture

Lea Shaver

Yale UNIVERSITY PRESS

New Haven & London

Published with assistance from the foundation established in memory of Amasa Stone Mather of the Class of 1907, Yale College.

Set in Janson type by IDS Infotech Ltd.
Printed in the United States of America.

ISBN 978-0-300-22600-3 (hardcover : alk. paper)
Library of Congress Control Number: 2019941035
A catalogue record for this book is available from the British Library.

This paper meets the requirements of ANSI/NISO Z39.48-1992 (Permanence of Paper).

10 9 8 7 6 5 4 3 2 1

Contents

Contents

Ending Book Hunger

Book Hunger

"Half the world suffers from hunger. The other half wants to lose weight." So read a slogan I once saw chalked on a campus sidewalk. Its irony was aimed at the global food crisis, but the same paradox holds true for books. If you are reading this book, you almost surely belong to the latter group. As readers in a world of abundance, you and I struggle to manage our textual diets in the limited time we have. Amazon.com now offers more than a million titles for instant digital delivery. Whether we use a library, a bookstore, or a digital device, our main challenge is choosing among all the appetizing options.

For most of the world's population, however, things are very different. In the 1980s, economic crises across

Africa sparked desperate shortages of food and many other goods, including books. It was in this context that writers first began to speak of the continent as suffering from a "book famine." Yet the problem was not limited to that decade; books were always too scarce, and still are. Today, many countries in sub-Saharan Africa still cannot provide a textbook for every student. While book hunger is most severe in Africa, it remains a problem in every region of the world. Asia's four billion residents speak more than 2,300 languages, but only a minority of these have active publishing industries. Most cities in Brazil have no bookstores, although the Latin American country is one of the world's largest economies.

Over the past several decades, governments around the world have made great strides in expanding opportunities for primary education and ending illiteracy. More than 90 percent of the world's young adults possess basic literacy, defined as the ability to read and write a simple sentence in any language. Unfortunately, half of them still lack access to the reading materials necessary to make this skill truly life-changing. For around one billion children, a hunger for books is holding back their education—their best hope for escaping from poverty. Three billion adults remain impacted by their childhood experience with book hunger. This is more than half of the world's population.

Book hunger is also a serious issue for lower-income families in the United States. In a survey conducted in 2016 for the "Read Aloud 15 Minutes" national campaign, 93 percent of American parents agreed with the statement, "It is a parent's responsibility to begin teaching their child how to read on their own." Many parents reported difficulty in obtaining books, however, with half complaining that children's books are too expensive. The Forum on Child and Family Statistics reports that four out of every ten American children live in families that have trouble paying for basic needs like food, shelter, and clothing. For families below the poverty line, maintaining a private book collection that grows with the child is an investment they cannot afford.

The Importance of Books

Whether in paper or digital format, books play a very special role in our literary diets. Their longer form provides a unique opportunity to explore ideas and stories in depth. More so than newspapers, blog posts, or social media, books challenge us to expand our horizons of knowledge and imagination. They offer opportunities to acquire tools and concepts we can put to use in our personal lives, our communities, and our businesses. Philosopher Martha Nussbaum has identified reading and self-expression as among the fundamental capabilities that every person should be enabled to exercise. She emphasizes that education, through engagement with texts, is central for critical thinking, world citizenship, and imaginative understanding. In the words of one of George R. R. Martin's characters, "A mind needs books as a sword needs a whetstone, if it is to keep its edge."

While the importance of access to nonfiction works such as textbooks and reference books may be most obvious, books of all types are vital. Many of life's most important lessons are conveyed most effectively in a story. Novelist Neil Gaiman argues persuasively that fiction serves a particularly powerful need as a vehicle for cultivating social imagination. Novels and personal memoirs cultivate the ability to relate to and empathize with people different from ourselves. Science fiction encourages the imagination and creativity from which technological innovation grows. Nonfiction enables adults to keep learning and growing beyond their formal education. Short stories and novels develop the advanced literacy skills that people need to succeed in formal education and to make use of text-based informational resources. For children, picture books and chapter books are essential steps on the path to advanced literacy, as well as opportunities for emotional growth.

An extensive body of research demonstrates that a book-rich environment is critical to a child's educational achievement and future income. The "book effect" has been demonstrated in countries both rich and poor, communist and capitalist, and across diverse cultures. Sociologists Mariah Evans, Jonathan Kelley, and Joanna Sikora reviewed studies on the relationship between books and life outcomes from forty-two countries. They found that even the smallest of home book collections benefit children, and these benefits increase with the size of the collection. Growing up in a home with at least two hundred books promotes a child's future success more powerfully than having parents with college degrees. This rigorous body of research proves what those of us who grew up with books already know. Children who read regularly for pleasure become fluent readers, take joy in learning, and perform well in school.

In the United States, book hunger strikes hardest during summer break. Researchers have known for more than a decade that students of all socioeconomic levels develop their reading skills similarly in school. What happens in the summer, however, produces a profound achievement gap. Students from middle- and higher-income families continue to steadily improve their reading skills, but those from lower-income families do not. "Summer vacations created a gap of about 3 months between middle- and lower-class students," according to a meta-analysis by Harris Cooper and colleagues. Researchers such as Richard Allington, Julie Au, Doris Entwisle, Gary Evans, Stephen Krashen, Jim Lindsay, Anne McGill-Franzen, Jeff McQuillan, Fay Shin, and Nicole Whitehead have all drawn the connection between summer reading and access to books.

An experiment by Richard Allington and colleagues served to clearly demonstrate this effect. First- through fourth-graders from high-poverty schools participated in the study. Half were randomly selected to participate in a book fair, where they could choose ten books to take home for the summer. Simply receiving ten books, with no further intervention, led to greater summer reading. Over three years, reading achievement scores among this group noticeably improved compared to a matched group of students who were not given books. Modest interventions to encourage students to read their books more frequently can further strengthen the effect. No amount of urging will have an impact, however, if the child cannot get access to appropriate books.

The Limits of Commercial Publishing

Markets have worked astoundingly well at producing and delivering an ever expanding variety of novels, textbooks, nonfiction, and children's books for affluent English speakers. You and I have book collections that would be the envy of kings and queens from an earlier age. Low-income readers, however, are largely priced out. Like health care, education, and car seats, books are what economists would call "merit goods." It is socially desirable for everyone to have access to them, but this can only be achieved through subsidies or free provision. Economic theory predicts (accurately) that markets will form to produce many merit goods. Without charitable and government support, however, many people will be excluded.

Book hunger is particularly resistant to market solutions because of the extreme diversity of products readers need. Economist Joel Waldfogel explains that markets work best when large numbers of people want the same things, but they are likely to fail to serve consumers with less common preferences. A vaccine developed for insured patients in Paris can also be used by residents of remote villages in India. The same is not true with books. The book market especially fails at producing diverse books for cultural minorities, accessible books for readers with blindness or dyslexia, and books in disadvantaged languages.

Consider the Zulu language, which is spoken by ten million people in South Africa. The vast majority of Zulu speakers are literate. Every day, Zulu newspapers sell hundreds of thousands of copies. With an average house-hold income around $5,000 U.S., however, very few Zulu speakers can afford to purchase books. As a logical conse-quence, the Zulu book publishing industry is next to non-existent. The Publishers' Association of South Africa counts only seven hundred Zulu books currently in print. The vast majority of these are children's books produced with charitable and government subsidies for use by schools. Because Zulu is not widely spoken outside of South Africa, this is not just a national total, but also a global one.

Some economists would say that the market's failure to produce more books in Zulu and other disadvantaged languages proves that there is no real demand for such books. Yet poor consumers also buy fewer cars and coats, and we do not scratch our heads and wonder why. No one imagines that the poor simply do not wish to drive cars, or that they have some sort of cultural preference for being cold. Like driving a car and dressing warmly, read-ing costs money, and not everyone has it.

A parallel problem exists in book publishing and drug development. Public health experts refer to tropical epi-demics like leprosy, sleeping sickness, river blindness, dengue fever, and Guinea worm disease as "neglected dis-eases." Collectively, these diseases and others like them trap one billion people in poverty. Yet drug companies have no financial incentive to produce treatments for them, because the diseases are overwhelmingly concentrated among the global poor. Those who need the product cannot afford to pay for it. Those who can afford to pay for the product do not need it. Similarly, commercial publishers have no incentive to produce books for "neglected languages." The biggest profits lie in publishing for global languages spoken by hundreds of millions of potential buyers. Smaller profits can be made in national languages whose speakers are generally affluent, such as Dutch, Swedish, Hebrew, and Korean. Where a language's speakers are predominantly poor, however, the economics of publishing simply do not bear out.

Market failure does not mean that book hunger is an unsolvable problem. It simply means that we must look to charitable and public approaches to pick up where markets leave off. We must begin to think about books in the same way we think of education and health care. Market, charitable, and government efforts are all needed, or too many people will be left out. Indeed, this has long been the case. Philanthropists founded public libraries in the nineteenth and twentieth centuries to bring the luxury of reading within reach of the common man. By themselves, however, libraries cannot achieve this goal. Children's television programming comes straight to the home, with hundreds of options available at no direct cost. Books must become similarly convenient if they are to compete effectively for children's time. Libraries also have very limited reach in most of the world, are expensive to run, and are limited to purchasing titles already in print. In the twenty-first century, more innovative approaches are needed.

Why and How to Read This Book

Ending Book Hunger is intended for publishers, writers, artists, librarians, teachers, philanthropists, policymakers, nonprofit leaders, and anyone else interested in how to turn "the right to read" into a reality. My goal is to give readers from every field a clear picture of nonprofit publishing as an emerging field of social enterprise.

One of the best-known examples of social enterprise is the microlending model pioneered by Bangladeshi economics professor Mohammed Yunus and the Grameen Bank. Microfinance lifts living standards among the very poor by providing women with tiny loans to start or expand their own microenterprises. Because this model generates a return on investment, it has been able to expand to serve over 200 million families in three decades. To achieve this, however, Yunus and his fellow social entrepreneurs had to innovate solutions to every problem that had kept traditional banks from effectively serving this population. As the microlending example demonstrates, social enterprise can be transformative when it introduces a new business model to deliver a socially important product or service that is effective, sustainable, and scalable.

My research convinces me that a similar potential exists in efforts to end book hunger. Mainstream publishing models currently reach a tiny fraction of all people, while newer models hold the potential to serve many times more. The nonprofits profiled here represent the cutting edge of this innovation. They are laser focused on developing new models of book development and distribution because they understand that innovation is essential to their mission. While book hunger affects readers of all ages, existing nonprofit efforts are almost entirely focused on serving children. Most of this book therefore focuses on nonprofits promoting access to children's literature. This is sensible as a starting point, both because this is where charitable dollars flow most freely and because adults will not read books if they did not learn to as children. The underlying innovations, however, can also be applied to trade publishing for adults.

The first half of this book offers an in-depth, detailed survey of the state of the art in nonprofit publishing.

Through my conversations with nonprofit leaders, I have identified four major challenges that all efforts to address book hunger must overcome. These include: reaching readers who cannot afford the going prices, serving a more diverse population, developing new titles in neglected languages, and developing more cost-effective distribution methods, both in print and digitally. These challenges are developed in Chapters 2 through 5. In each of these chapters, I will introduce you to nonprofits that are doing a particularly good job at addressing these challenges and explore what we can learn from their efforts.

Of course, any publisher wishing to tap into the vast potential market of people who do not yet buy books must address these same four challenges. Organizations focused on social impact rather than profit simply have a greater sense of urgency. They cannot accomplish their institutional mission unless they find solutions to these persistent challenges. This pushes them to devote greater resources to experimentation and to take on the significant risk of trial and error. As social entrepreneurs figure out new techniques to serve their target readers, mainstream publishers and booksellers should find it profitable to imitate their tactics.

The second half of the book proposes several ways to further increase the impact of nonprofit publishing. I begin by explaining why nonprofits find it so challenging to secure copyright permissions from publishers. I then explore five possible solution spaces. These include: more coordinated approaches to granting permissions, relying on copyright law's fair use exception, enacting new exceptions to address book hunger, using Creative Commons licenses to encourage sharing, and leveraging non-monetary incentives for authorship. Although I write from my background as an expert in copyright law, I assume that most of my readers have no prior knowledge of law. These chapters rely heavily on storytelling and concrete examples to keep the main ideas and proposals clear and memorable.

The creativity of social entrepreneurs is fascinating and inspiring, but we cannot simply celebrate their accomplishments. Difficult questions must also be asked. Nonprofit publishers and book dealers are now serving tens of millions of readers—but this is just 1 percent of the world's book-hungry population. How can this effort scale up to produce and distribute enough books to meet the enormous social need? With this grand challenge in mind, the book concludes by sketching out a highly cost-effective model that could end book hunger for a billion children by 2030. My research leads me to the conclusion that a mass translation effort offers the most cost-effective approach to title creation. On the distribution side, nonprofit approaches can have even greater impact if digital distribution is used effectively. For print copies, nonprofit efforts should be supplemented by commercial and government approaches. I believe, however, that a problem this large requires many good ideas and even more helping hands. Whether you are a publisher, author, illustrator, educator, bookseller, librarian, or any other kind of book lover, I invite you to join an important public conversation about how we can overcome barriers and finally bring books to billions of new readers.

TWO

Making Books Affordable

Country music star Dolly Parton is a woman of many accomplishments: actress, musician, entrepreneur, and philanthropist. At heart, however, Dolly is a poet. Her lyrics are recognized across America and beyond, including such favorites as "I Will Always Love You," "9 to 5," and "Jolene." As might be expected, Dolly Parton is also a voracious reader, with an extensive book collection. As a child growing up in Appalachia, however, Dolly experienced book hunger first-hand.

In an interview with the *Boston Globe*, the singer-songwriter described the role of books in her own childhood. "We weren't allowed to bring schoolbooks home, not even for homework, because all of us kids—there were

12 of us—would tear them up, chew them up, get food on them. Daddy couldn't afford to replace the schoolbooks if we ruined them." Although her father could not read or write, Dolly's mother taught her to read from the one book the family owned. "My mother's Bible was the book that was always there. We knew better than to mess with that." Dolly's own childhood experience motivated her to found the Imagination Library as a way to ensure that all children could experience the joy of book ownership.

The Imagination Library

Like Dolly herself, the philanthropic project had humble beginnings. At Christmastime in 1995, the Dollywood Foundation mailed its first shipment of books to the children of Sevier County, Tennessee. Today, the Dolly Parton Imagination Library delivers new books by mail to one million children each month, in the United States and Canada, the United Kingdom and Australia. The organization has delivered more than 100 million books.

Dolly Parton's Imagination Library works to ensure that all young children can enjoy a home environment rich in books, regardless of family income. With the help of community partners and local fundraising, the organization mails a new book each month to every participating child, ages zero to five. Importantly, there is absolutely no cost to the parents to participate in the Imagination Library. Nor do parents have to make a special effort to go out and obtain the books. They simply appear in the mailbox on a regular basis. Parents have to give permission, provide their address, and give the ages of their children.

The first book every child receives is *The Little Engine that Could,* and the last is *Kindergarten, Here I Come!* The titles in between vary each year. A panel selects a list of lovely, delightful picture books appropriate for each year of the child's life. By age five, a participating child will have up to sixty books of her own. Families with more than one child will have an even larger variety of titles, since portions of the book list change each year.

Ensuring access to books is not only about improving educational outcomes and enhancing future job prospects. Stories also inspire, and may help an impoverished reader to envision optimistic narratives for his or her own life. Dolly often says that her favorite book as a child was Watty Piper's *The Little Engine that Could.* "I think that little book had a big impact on me, on my big dreams. I still have that philosophy. I am a little engine that did." Reading and owning books allows people to see themselves as educated, intelligent, and capable of life-long learning. "If you can read you can educate yourself," Dolly told the *Boston Globe*. If you can't go to school or don't want to, you can still go buy a book about any subject you want and educate yourself." Although others often describe the Imagination Library as a literacy charity, the organization does not see itself that way. Its mission statement expresses a broader ambition: "to inspire children to dream more, learn more, care more, be more." Books are simply the vehicle for this effort to lift people up.

Related to this emphasis on dignity, the Imagination Library has never required families to state or prove that they qualify as low-income. From the beginning, the program was open to all children in the community, whether their families were rich or poor. C.E.O. David Dotson explains, "We are a universal program. Everyone in the community has to be eligible." It was important to Dolly to avoid stigmatizing children by singling them out as poor and therefore deserving of charity. "Being labeled as poor means being labeled as not as intelligent, not as ambitious, a victim in some way, all those stereotypes," Dotson explains.

Dotson often refers to this as the question of, "What are the terms of the transaction? When we give the books, what do we want the kids to feel and not feel?" The Imagination Library strives to ensure that the book program makes participating children feel special, to uplift them rather than to shame them. Although many smaller book charities rely on second-hand books or "remaindered" books, Imagination Library has always insisted on new books, hand-selected for high quality by a panel of experts. Each book is presented as a personal gift from Dolly Parton, addressed to the children by name and delivered to their home mailbox.

Social Class and Access to Books

My own children—little girls ages eight, four, and two—have a home library embarrassing in its riches. Our friends and relatives can afford to purchase a twenty-dollar book as a gift on a special occasion or even "just because." They do so on the understanding that our family's more basic needs—for food, clothing, housing, and health care—are already securely met. In one week, my daughters received books as gifts from their grandparents, babysitter, and pediatrician. The same week, they also brought home used books from the daycare sharing shelf and the Little Free Library on our block. My daughters are fortunate to be growing up an environment of "book abundance," both in our home and in the larger community in which we live.

Other communities, however, are marked by "book scarcity." Professors Susan B. Neuman and Donna Celano inventoried books across four Philadelphia neighborhoods for their influential study titled "Access to Print in Low-Income and Middle-Income Communities." They found that poor neighborhoods had few stores selling books, and these were mostly cheap coloring books. "In these low-income neighborhoods, children would find it difficult, if not impossible, to purchase a book of any quality in local stores; in the middle-income neighborhoods, children would find it hard to escape them." Although children in the poor neighborhoods depended more heavily on public institutions for access to books, their libraries had shorter hours, lower-quality books, and more dilapidated facilities.

David Dotson, the Dollywood Foundation's president, emphasizes economic realities as the primary reason many children's homes have no books. "Cost is the number one issue, from our experience." For families with significant disposable income, books seem very affordable. It is possible to buy a Kindle for less than fifty dollars, and to add a wide selection of e-books for just ten dollars per month. Yet at least 40 percent of American children live in households that do not earn enough to easily cover basic needs. Says Dotson, "Books are expensive, and the cost is prohibitive, because it seems and feels like a luxury when you're worried about food and utilities and car payment and being laid off." For these families, books can be too valuable even to borrow, because parents cannot afford to replace lost books or pay late fees. In my hometown of Indianapolis, for instance, a seven-year-old who is two weeks late in returning ten picture books would owe fourteen dollars in library fines.

First Book

Other organizations have also set their sights on the problem of book affordability. First Book, based in Washington, D.C., has a staff of seventy-five people, delivering low-cost new books to a national network of more than 170,000 classrooms and nonprofit organizations serving children from low-income families. The organization's mission is overcoming what its website flags as "the number one barrier to book ownership—affordability."

Rather than mailing books directly to homes, First Book follows a business-to-business model, partnering with other organizations serving children from low-income households. Even when family budgets may be too tight, schools, classrooms, and community organizations often do have some resources they can spend on book purchasing. These may include federal Title I funds, program budgets, the proceeds from a fundraiser, or a teacher's personal money. First Book helps stretch those resources further, by offering books to eligible purchasers at up to 90 percent off normal retail prices.

First Book began by tackling the logistical challenges of warehousing, shipping, and online ordering to make better use of leftover books donated by publishers. This system enabled member organizations to select exactly the titles they wanted, while paying just for shipping and handling. Thus, a classroom can obtain books at just the right reading level, on themes related to a particular topic, and can give every child a copy of the same book when appropriate. More recently, the group introduced the First Book Marketplace, which sells new books at a 50–90 percent discount. This online bookstore is accessible only to teachers and organizations serving low-income children. A hardback copy of the Caldecott Honor book *The Adventures of Beekle: An Unimaginary Friend*, which normally sells for $17.99, costs just $6.20 for First Book members. Many books sell for $2 or less. Even at these low prices, publishers earn a profit on Marketplace sales. Most recently, First Book has introduced a digital lending program as well, in which qualified children can borrow e-books for up to two months at a time, at no cost to the child or to the partner organization.

Driving Down Costs

Though First Book and Imagination Library have very different delivery models, they leverage many of the same cost-cutting strategies. These include contracting directly with publishers for custom print runs, ordering in high volume with no returns, relying on paperback copies, and delivering these in bundles through the postal system. These lessons can be useful for other organizations seeking to follow in their footsteps. Imagination Library's model works best for younger children who are not yet in school. First Book's model works best for older children who may be more selective in what they want to read.

Perhaps most important, both organizations contract directly with book publishers. Imagination Library has its book orders custom printed—either domestically or in Asia—and trucked to Knoxville, Tennessee. The books are then bulk mailed by a partner company. First Book also relies on the postal system to fulfill online orders. Neither organization pays book wholesalers, brokers, or retailers. This allows publishers to offer a lower price per book, while still realizing a profit.

Both organizations are also in a unique position to guarantee publishers a very high volume of sales. Imagination Library works with only eight different titles per month, for a total of around seventy-five titles per year. By limiting its selection, the organization is able to purchase up to 300,000 copies of each title. Because printers charge much less on a per-book basis for large orders, the publisher can lower the price for a high-volume buyer and still make a good profit. First Book delivers around twenty million books to three million students each year.

Apart from volume, both organizations also offer publishers another attractive term: no returns. A typical bookstore might agree to accept one hundred copies, but it reserves the right to return any copies that do not sell. This makes printing books a somewhat risky business; a publisher that prints too many copies could lose money on that title. With Imagination Library and First Book, there are no "remainders" to deal with. Imagination Library knows exactly how many copies it needs, because it pushes specific books to a known quantity of readers. Although consumer choice is very important to First Book, the organization is committed to moving all the books it receives. Perl explains: "We purchase the books on a non-refundable basis. We emphasize to publishers, we want them to profit from working with us, even if it is a slim margin."

Imagination Library purchases exclusively from one publisher. This allows the organization to negotiate even lower prices and to consolidate shipping expenses. President David Dotson explains, "Penguin gives us great prices and logistical flexibility. We are able to customize the books, manipulate the book format that makes it most affordable to mail." There are also organizational efficiencies to working exclusively with one publishing partner. "If you have a problem, you have one dedicated team that can solve any problem. With five publishers, you would have more problems." First Book works with a diverse group of publishers, however, to maintain much more diverse offerings of more than five thousand different titles at a time.

As might be expected, both organizations also save money by purchasing most of their books in paperback. Children's books generally sell better in hardcover, which is preferred by gift givers and by libraries. Paperback copies, however, are less expensive both to print and to mail. A publisher that might otherwise be selling a particular title only in hardcover may agree to produce a special run of paperback copies for a charitable distributor. This reduces publishers' concerns that low-cost copies will find their way to the second-hand market and drive down sales revenue.

One strategy neither organization uses is relying exclusively on donated books. Although book publishers can earn a tax deduction for donating excess copies, First Book and the Imagination Library see advantages to purchasing exactly the books they want. Dotson explains,

"Consistency, dependability, quality—we could not reliably achieve that if we were relying upon charitable generosity. We didn't want to use remaindered books that no one else in the country bought. We wanted to build a business model that made it affordable and replicable and increased the quality and ensured the reliability and developed the relationship that allowed for customizing it." Although First Book continues to accept remainders, the organization moves a much higher volume of books through the sale of new copies.

Organizations like First Book and Imagination Library are reinventing the traditional book supply chain. Rather than relying on for-profit bookstores as an intermediary, both have innovated alternative, more cost-effective systems to deliver books to children from low-income backgrounds. In the Imagination Library model, just $120 in local fundraising enables children to receive sixty books, while Dolly Parton's foundation covers organizational overhead. Both organizations manage to source and deliver books at a 50–90 percent markdown from typical prices. Through a combination of charitable dollars and cost savings, innovative nonprofits are bringing books to millions of American children who otherwise could not afford them.

THREE

Reflecting Diversity

When they were four and seven, my eldest two daughters adored the book *Underpants Dance*, by Marlena Zapf. The story is both funny and sweet, celebrating a preschooler's socially inappropriate passion for showing off her "fancy, lacy, lovely underpants." What makes this book so beloved in our family is my girls' personal identification with the characters. Like my little Eleanor, the book's younger sister delights in being the center of attention. The book's older sister is much more serious, and easily embarrassed, just like my older daughter Josephine. Lynne Avril's illustrations of the two sisters—skinny with short, curly blonde hair—even look like my daughters. In fact, when I would read this book aloud at bedtime, my daughters insisted that I replace the characters' names with their own. Though written as a story about Lily and Marigold McBloom, in our home it became a story about Ellie and Jozi Shaver.

From our family's perspective, *Underpants Dance* is a fantastic book, but what about for a different child? Of thirty people depicted in this book, all but four are white. This is quite a significant underrepresentation of America's diversity. Non-white and mixed-raced children are now a majority among children seven and under. In this story, however, none of the people of color are important enough to have names. They serve only as a sprinkling of color in the background. The book's settings and events also reflect a distinctly upper-middle-class lifestyle. The McBloom sisters play on a suburban lawn, ride in the family car, attend ballet lessons, visit an art museum, and try on new clothes as if they were a burden rather than a blessing. How would such a story be received by a child whose family struggles to meet basic needs?

Windows and Mirrors

There is nothing wrong with any single children's book being culturally specific to a white, upper-income, American experience. The problem is that this pattern is so strong that children's literature as a whole is systematically less attractive or even alienating to children who do not fit that mold. Since 2012, most children born in America belong to a racial or ethnic minority group (Latino, African American, Asian, Native American, biracial, or multiracial). Yet only 7.5 percent of children's books published that year prominently featured minority characters, according to the University of Wisconsin Cooperative Children's Book Center. The center began tracking such data in 1985, after its founder realized with shock that only eighteen out of twenty-five hundred children's books published that year had been written or illustrated by an African-American creator. For nearly three decades, progress in improving the diversity of children's book authors, illustrators, and characters was limited. After reaching an all-time high of 13 percent in 2007, the appearance of minority characters declined again for many years.

In a seminal survey of children's literature from the 1960s and '70s, *Shadow and Substance*, Professor Rudine Sims Bishop argued that stories about black Americans tended to fit three types. A first wave of "social conscience" books by white authors sought to educate white children in modern liberal values, yet often reinforced racial stereotypes. The next wave of "melting pot" books began to feature characters (either major or minor) who were incidentally black, but rarely reflected distinctly African-

American experiences. A third wave began to feature everyday experiences that black children can relate to, while celebrating cultural distinctiveness. This vein of "culturally conscious" children's literature emerged in the 1970s, driven by a new generation of African-American authors.

Bishop's theoretical framework and literary analysis powerfully informed the next several decades of scholarship, authorship, and publishing. This proved true not only for African-American children's literature, but also for later-emerging genres of Native-American, Latino, and Asian-American children's books. Today, Bishop's framework has been extended to include children's books reflecting diversity of disability, sexual orientation, gender identity, and social class. Publishers, authors, teachers, and librarians still commonly invoke Bishop's concept of "windows and mirrors" to express the idea that all children need and deserve to see both themselves and others in books. Bishop's own poetic articulation of this concept deserves quoting at length:

> Books are sometimes windows, offering views of worlds that may be real or imagined, familiar or strange. These windows are also sliding glass doors, and readers have only to walk through in imagination. . . . When lighting conditions are just right, however, a window can also be a mirror. Literature transforms human experience and reflects it back to us, and in that reflection we can see

our own lives and experiences as part of the larger human experience.

As Bishop suggests, cultural diversity in children's literature is particularly important for the education of minority children, but also has an important impact on white children. Repeated exposure to media that sensitively depicts racial and cultural differences helps all children to empathize and identify across difference. Conversely, a media diet that systematically celebrates white characters as central, while marginalizing nonwhite characters, may reinforce ideologies of white supremacy in subtle but deeply problematic ways. Representation of gender, disability, sexual orientation, and social class in children's books has similar implications. As the African-American author Walter Dean Myers wrote for the *New York Times:* "Books transmit values. They explore our common humanity. What is the message when some children are not represented in those books?"

We Need Diverse Books

It began as a hashtag movement. In early 2014, BookCon launched as an annual meeting place for authors and fans of children's books. The authors announced as speakers and panelists were all white. Authors and readers of color were appalled. A group created #weneeddiversebooks in protest.

"People wrote their own reasons, included photos of themselves, and posted on social media," explains Nicole A. Johnson. The campaign triggered "a groundswell of interest and demand and advocacy around diversity in children's literature." Authors, illustrators, booksellers, publishers, librarians, teachers, and community leaders began to exchange book lists and advocacy strategies. The campaign went viral, led to an online fundraiser, and eventually became a registered nonprofit. Johnson, initially attracted by the social media campaign, now serves as the organization's executive director.

Today, We Need Diverse Books works on a slim budget to raise consciousness through social media campaigns, book awards, classroom events, and programs to support diverse new authors, illustrators, editors, and other publishing professionals. The organization defines diversity broadly, including dimensions of race, ethnicity, gender, disability, religion, and sexual orientation. Among the unique initiatives of the organization is an app named OurStory. The tool features a curated selection of diverse titles, searchable along any of these criteria. This enables librarians, teachers, and parents to easily identify books reflecting the experiences of any child.

"Every human being deserves to be able to see themselves in the stories they read," affirms author Caroline

Tung Richmond, cofounder of We Need Diverse Books. As a child, young Caroline Tung never had that experience. In high school, however, her English teacher assigned passages from *The Joy Luck Club*. The novel resonated deeply with her own experiences growing up with parents and grandparents who had immigrated to the United States. "It was like Amy Tan had reached into my head and pulled out my own memories and put them in a book." The experience was profound. "That moment was when I first felt seen and heard."

Nicole Johnson, the organization's executive director, tells a similar story. "I didn't find my first book that I really connected with until college." In an African-American literature class, she discovered authors whose books she truly related to, like Audre Lorde and Octavia Butler. "Especially J. California Cooper. Her characters really spoke in the voice of my family." After college, Johnson ran summer reading programs in urban communities. The books chosen for use in the program reflected the ethnic identities of the participating children. "To introduce that to kids when they were five and six was just amazing."

As an African-American parent of biracial children, Johnson views diverse books as particularly important to personal growth. "This includes racial diversity about people of color as sheroes and heroes, so young people can be inspired by people in their community. There is also a turn among contemporary writers to create characters that build imagination and wonder," Johnson continues. "Say a young African-American girl is a hero in the story, that is not necessarily a story about racial justice, but that still has a message of empowerment and growth." Johnson believes these messages are especially important for children who experience discrimination on the basis of identity. "It signals to young people that you are not just your oppression. You are also an artist, a musician, you are bright and creative. You can be a princess; you can be Harry Potter."

Richmond also emphasizes the power of seeing the world from someone else's perspective. "Even if it's a fictional character, it's about understanding where that person is coming from, how that person grew up, how they act." For this reason, diverse books can help to bridge gaps of understanding between groups. Richmond points to the first recipient of the organization's Walter Dean Myers award as an example: *All American Boys* is a work of young adult fiction that focuses on the problem of police brutality. The book was cowritten in two narratives, one told from the perspective of a white teenager, the other a black teenager. "It speaks to what is going on in America right now," Richmond notes, "and it can help kids to find a personal angle to view it."

Stories for All

First Book, the charitable book dealer profiled in the previous chapter, also strives to ensure that children's books better reflect the diverse readers they serve. "What we realized about the lack of diversity is that it's quite undermining to literacy," says Kyle Zimmer, chief executive of First Book. "Kids want to read about themselves, it gives them perspective on who they are, encourages them to be proud of their heritage. And it teaches all of us empathy and tolerance. All of us ought to be reading about all of us."

Indeed, when First Book surveyed its network of literacy organizations, 90 percent of respondents expressed a strong interest in more diverse books. Yet such books were difficult to find in most bookstores and on most publishers' lists. So First Book leveraged its unique position as a major buyer to channel the grassroots demand for diverse books. The charity pledged to purchase $500,000 worth of books from the publisher that offered the best selection of diverse books at affordable prices. Twenty-six bids were entered. First Book ultimately selected two winners, spending $1 million and adding 650 diverse new titles to its offerings. The effort also made an important point by drawing attention to First Book's market power and its preference for diverse content.

First Book also hand-picks particular titles from diverse authors who have yet to be published. For each "new voices" title selected, First Book purchases ten thousand copies. This advance purchasing commitment helps new authors launch their writing careers on a strong footing. It also helps publishers mitigate the risk involved in launching an unknown author. "By making those books viable at First Book, it allows the publishers to step out with more confidence," says Zimmer. "They know some part of their baseline investment is covered. When they stick somebody out there and their books don't sell, they take an economic hit."

To achieve real change, Zimmer argues, you have to appreciate the economics of book publishing. "Publishing is a consignment-based industry," she explains. "The retail price of books is artificially elevated, because the publishers have to cover all the books that are going to come back to them." A premium picture book retails for fifteen to twenty dollars in the United States. "The people who can afford on a regular basis to buy those books are about the top 5–10 percent of the socioeconomic ladder," Zimmer continues. "In the U.S. right now, the profile of those people is white. That is the reality in the market today." Publishers that are trying to introduce new voices and perspectives in the marketplace, Zimmer says, "are trying to break through into a monolithic consumer base." For a commercial publisher, this mission conflicts with the profit motive. "The color that the publishers care most about is green."

Nicole Johnson of We Need Diverse Books expresses a differing view. "I think to just rest the cause on economics is to avoid a real conversation about who's running the industry. Where is the diversity among booksellers? Where are the diverse voices within [literacy nonprofits]? We should be placing questions of racism and poverty at the center of the conversation." She also bemoans the assumption that a book written by an African-American author about an African-American character would appeal only to African-American readers. "There is an implicit bias there that says these books are not worthy, they are not welcome, and therefore the people that wrote them and read them are not welcome." She points out that publishers specializing in diverse books have found it sustainable and viable to do so. "Within the publishing industry there are very successful examples of how placing racial diversity and identity at the center of your work can actually be sustainable. It depends on publishers being more intentional about what they create and curate" and how they invest in marketing it.

Her colleague Caroline Tung Richmond goes on to point out other ways in which social and structural racism contribute to low diversity in publishing, tied to a different sort of economics. "It's an apprentice-based industry. An editorial assistant will be lucky to get paid $30,000 a year, but they have to live in New York City." Early in a publishing career, she points out, junior professionals "need help from a partner or family who can subsidize their rent, their utilities, their transportation. Only a narrow slice of the population can afford to break into the industry and stay in it." Recognizing this problem, We Need Diverse Books created a grant program for diverse publishing interns "to give them a boost that their counterparts might be getting from their family." Interns may work as editors, marketing associates, or in sales. The program also helps to raise awareness in the industry of the need for more diversity in hiring. To participate in the internship program, publishing partners must also commit to pay their interns. Johnson points out: "Our award is supplement to the salary they receive for the summer. That is a structural shift in how the publishers manage interns. That goes beyond our work, that opens the door for many more people to enter the field."

The two organizations' combination of awareness raising, market influence, and talent development has had a noticeable impact, according to more recent data from the University of Wisconsin's Cooperative Children's

Book Center. Between 2012 and 2018, the portion of U.S. children's books written or illustrated by creators of color went from 6.3 percent to 22.9 percent of all new titles. Books prominently featuring characters of color also more than tripled, going from 7.5 percent to 27.4 percent of new children's titles. These dramatic results over just a six-year period demonstrate the potential for well-designed nonprofit efforts to push commercial publishers in a new direction.

PJ Library

While First Book and We Need Diverse Books take a broad approach to diversity, PJ Library occupies a specific niche. This charity follows a fundraising and distribution model based on Dolly Parton's Imagination Library. Each year, the organization distributes about 2.2 million books to more than 200,000 children across the United States and Canada. PJ Library is pleased to have a positive impact on literacy in young children. Its primary motivation, however, is to preserve and promote Jewish cultural traditions. The PJ Library selection committee asks some of the same questions any publisher or librarian of children's books would ask: Is this story suitable to the age group? Is it engaging for both children and parents? Will children want to enjoy this book over and over? They also ask questions that are unique to the content-based mission of the organization: "Is the content appropriate to the PJ Library mission, and does the book contain a message of strong Jewish values?" "Does the book reflect historical Jewish life, contemporary Jewish life, or some valuable aspect of the Jewish experience?" and "Will this book prompt family discussions about Jewish topics and lead families to make Jewish choices?"

The organization uses a variety of strategies to source books meeting these criteria. Because there is already a significant tradition of Jewish children's publishing in the United States, PJ Library is able to choose many appropriate titles from trade publishers' existing lists. The charity has also commissioned new editions of at least twenty out-of-print titles. Kar-Ben Publishing specializes in Jewish children's titles, with a backlist of more than 750 such books. "They are a fifth of our list," reports PJ Library's Samara Klein. "And it's a very symbiotic relationship. They publish what we need and we buy what they publish." The organization also maintains strategic partnerships with more than 50 other publishers, both big and small.

PJ Library's existence is also shaping the operation of for-profit publishing in the niche of Jewish children's books. In particular, there are books of more marginal interest to the for-profit market that PJ Library's existence helps to bring to print. A book on a lesser-known Jewish holiday, for example, might not be financially viable otherwise. Publishers sometimes contact PJ Library to find out if the charity would be interested in a title before deciding whether to sign an author.

PJ Library also encourages authors to submit manuscripts directly to its selection committee. If the committee likes a title, its chair will act as an agent for the book to find a publisher. The selection committee may give editorial suggestions to the author as part of this process. PJ Library also maintains a list of suggested concepts for books that can be consulted by potential authors. In these ways, PJ Library is performing the role typically performed by publishers, selecting which books will be published and editing those works for publication. PJ Library also performs an essential marketing role traditionally performed by publishers. PJ Library works to identify the audience for a particular book, and to inform that audience of that book's existence.

As PJ Library expands internationally, it finds itself pushed even further into the role of publishing original content. The organization's director of international publishing, Samara Klein, explained that as it enters other countries, such as Mexico and Russia, the North American model required adaptation. "In the Spanish market they are simply not publishing Jewish children's books. There are really none, that I can find," Klein explains. To meet the need, PJ Library commissions translations. Using books PJ Library has already distributed in English, selected titles are sent to the Hebrew University in Mexico for review, where a local selection committee chooses which books will work best for nearby communities. A linguist in Argentina double-checks the translations, in part to ensure that the Spanish is sufficiently international, so that the books will work throughout Latin America.

As the organization expanded to Russia, the model required tweaking yet again. "The communities are so different in each of these countries that the books can't be the same really," Klein cautions. "The books that will work in Mexico are not necessarily the books that will work in Russia." The literary culture also differs. "In Russia, there are already Jewish children's books. It is not completely lacking. They have the largest collection of any country that we have explored." Yet the scale of locally written works is not yet sufficient. The model of translating English-language books still seems to be an important component of the approach. This solution, however, did not prove as satisfactory to the Russian partners as it was to the Mexican partners. "It's important to the community there to have Russian-originated books,"

Klein relates. "To bring in solely American-authored translated books is not perceived as well there."

The international exchange of titles now goes in both directions. PJ Library's Israeli program, Sifriyat Pijama, has published in Hebrew and Arabic for more than ten years. "Children's literature is a more respected profession in Israel," notes international lead Lian Kimia. "Your top fiction writers on the adult side also write children's books, it's really honored. The way that children's literature plays a role in society and history-building and sharing knowledge is strong, although there is not the culture of owning tons and tons of books." Several titles originally published in Hebrew have found their way to American publishers through PJ Library's efforts.

The Chameleon That Saved Noah's Ark, by Yael Mochadsky, is one example. At the book's core is a story familiar across many cultures, to which a modern author has added a novel twist. The book's historical setting avoids elements that might make the story too culturally specific to any modern country. Illustrator Orit Bergman further globalizes the illustrations by depicting Noah's family as multiracial, with skin tones ranging from dark brown to light pink. Although Israeli children do not necessarily expect a colorful and detailed picture on every page, Bergman's work satisfies even the high expectations of the American market. All of these elements help the book to work well for nationally and ethnically diverse readers.

Diversity by Design

The three organizations highlighted in this chapter share a common motivation to promote diversity in children's literature, but pursue it in different ways. We Need Diverse Books follows a more classic advocacy model, waging social media campaigns, offering trainings, speaking out, and engaging professional networks. First Book sees itself as adopting a more market-driven approach, offering the prospect of massive purchases to encourage publishers to take greater risks. PJ Library gets more closely involved in the details of editorial decisions, playing a significant role in shaping the commercial publishing market within its niche.

Importantly, all three organizations see themselves as partnering closely with existing commercial publishers. They serve as consumer advocates, an intermediary between commercial publishers and their target communities. Based in the United States, these organizations happen to find themselves at the center of the world's largest publishing industry. They purchase from existing offerings, they push the publishers they buy from to develop new offerings, and they support those efforts by serving as an important source of income.

As the example of PJ Library illustrates, reflecting cultural diversity in book publishing is not just a national challenge, but also an international one. Organizations working to serve readers in the developing world, especially in Asia and Africa, face very similar challenges in sourcing culturally relevant books. These are complicated, however, by an even more basic challenge: overcoming the desperate shortage of books in most of the world's languages.

FOUR

Serving All Languages

Why are you reading this book in English? For native speakers, that question has a simple answer. English just happens to be the language you grew up hearing from your parents, your community, and your teachers. It is only natural that you would learn to read in English. This is, however, a privileged position to occupy. Many—perhaps even most—of the readers of this book are not native speakers of the language. They are among the half billion people in the world who have learned English through years of intensive study.

According to David Crystal, English is the most widely studied foreign language in the world. Since World War II, it has emerged as the dominant language of global commerce and culture. English now serves as the adopted common language of India, Pakistan, the Philippines, most of the African continent, and the United Nations. One-quarter of the world's population speaks English as a native or an acquired language.

Whether by chance or by choice, to be fluent in English greatly expands one's reading options. English accounts for 80 percent of the e-book titles available on Amazon.com, 80 percent of academic journals, and more than half of all content on the Internet. The dominance of English as a global publishing language is a chicken-and-egg story. Bilingual and multilingual writers often choose to publish in English to reach the widest possible audience. Publishers are more enthusiastic about investing in English-language titles because the potential market is so large. In turn, people clamor to learn English in large part because the language opens doors to so much cultural and reading material.

Neglected Languages

According to Ethnologue's *Languages of the World*, more than seven thousand languages are in use today. Nearly all have established writing systems, but only one in a hundred has a commercially viable publishing industry. English is the clear leader, accounting for twice as many books as Mandarin Chinese and German combined. Next follow three global imperialists: Spanish, French, and Russian. Rounding out the top of the list are national languages tied to particularly large economies: Portuguese (Brazil), Italian, Dutch (the Netherlands), Japanese, and Korean. Together, these eleven languages encompass just 22 percent of the world's population, but 83 percent of book publishing.

In the vast majority of languages, demographics and economics make publishing much less profitable. One billion people speak Hindi, making its publishing potential seem strong; but India's per capita income is only around U.S. $1,500. Educated Indians study English to gain access to books, and India's English-language book sales far outnumber its Hindi-language sales. A handful of other poor but populous languages have vibrant publishing scenes, although not lucrative ones: Arabic, Bengali, and Vietnamese, for instance. Many small but wealthy communities also do significant publishing, though not at significant profit. These include languages like Catalan, Danish, Dutch, Finnish, Icelandic, Hebrew, Norwegian and Swedish.

Unfortunately, the vast majority of the world's languages face the dual disadvantage of high poverty and small populations. While a children's book in the United

States might retail for ten to twenty dollars, publishers in Africa and most of Asia must sell books for only a dollar or two if they are to find buyers. It is virtually impossible to earn a return on investment at prices like this when volume is also low. A survey of children's publishing in Africa by Neil Butcher and associates concluded that profitable business models "simply do not exist" in low-income countries, "and the more marginalized the language, the less realistic this is." As a result, "The publishing of children's storybooks in most developing countries has tended to be a labour of love and commitment rather than a major business opportunity."

These economic realities result in very different opportunities for readers in different language communities. English has approximately one billion speakers, and represents the world's largest publishing market. English-speaking children can choose from approximately fifty-five thousand children's picture books currently in print. The world's sixth-largest language, Portuguese, has around 250 million speakers and is one of the world's top ten publishing markets. Yet there are only about two thousand picture books in print for Portuguese-speaking children. Moving further down the list, Zulu has ten million native speakers, making it the world's eighty-second largest language. Yet there are fewer than five hundred Zulu-language children's books in print. This is not even 1 percent of what is available to English-speaking children. For most languages, the situation is even worse. By my estimate, between 500 million and 1.25 billion children currently suffer from what I call extreme book hunger: in their languages, children's books are not available at any price. Melody Zavala, director of the Asia Foundation's Books for Asia program, explains: "In minority languages, which commercial publishing has no financial incentive to serve, you really have no books. Children are not learning in schools because they are being taught in languages that they do not understand." Organizations intent on improving education in neglected languages have had to grapple with this reality by becoming publishers themselves.

Room to Read

In Zambia, six-year-old Dabora scampers to a shelf in the brand-new library built at her government school. A bright green book has caught her eye. Written in Nyanja and attractively illustrated, its title is *Njala Nakolombo: Hunger Is a Monster.* The topic is something that Dabora has often dealt with in her life. Wide-eyed, little Dabora opens the book, puts her finger to the page, and begins to read. She reads fluently, her voice rising and falling, clearly enjoying the story. This book speaks to her, in her native tongue.

Nyanja is one of Zambia's seven official languages, the mother tongue of about four million people in the region. In line with internationally recommended educational practice, the children at this elementary school start their education by learning to read and write in their native language. In fourth grade, they will begin to study English. If they do well, they will continue to secondary education, which is taught exclusively in English. The school Dabora attends boasts new facilities, thanks to the American charity Room to Read. Room to Read provided a budget to stock the library shelves, and produced several original children's titles in Nyanja, including the one Dabora sits reading.

Not far away, Alisha Berger beams with pride at this "small miracle." A former children's book editor in New York, Berger now leads Room to Read's efforts to develop original picture books in the local languages for the communities Room to Read serves. She is in Zambia to see the fruits of their labors. Turning her attention from little Dabora, Berger scans the shelves of the newly stocked school library. There are about a thousand books, an enormous achievement, but the selection is not ideal. Locally purchased copies of British fairy tales like *Cinderella* and *Sleeping Beauty* feature heavily, supplemented by books donated from overseas, which are a mixture of great and not-so-great items. Almost nothing is culturally relevant. Almost everything is in English, which Dabora and her classmates barely speak. In the entire library, there are just ten books in the Nyanja language. All of these were published by Room to Read.

Better options are simply not available. Few children's titles have ever been produced in Zambian languages. Once published, they do not stay in print for long, and they can be impossible to find even a few years later. "I was really surprised to learn there was a series of Cambridge University–supported books in Zambian languages," Berger says. But "I can't find them, and nobody seems to know about them." This further contributes to the shortage of relevant titles a child like Dabora is able to access. Berger laments, "Given how my personal habit of reading has made my life incredibly rich with new ideas, worlds, and possibilities, it's hard to conceive of being Dabora, with not nearly enough books to feed her."

Room to Read started its own publishing program out of necessity. "Our organization's primary goal is really not to be a publisher," Berger explains. "We want to make sure that children have enough books to develop the skill and habit of reading. So we have fallen into publishing to fill a market gap." Since 2003, the heart of Room to Read's internal publishing effort has been early readers: short picture books that use compelling stories to introduce phonics and build fluency. The organization has now published more than thirteen hundred original children's book titles in thirty-two languages.

"In many countries where we work, there are almost no children's books," Berger says. "It is a matter of disposable income." As a result, "People haven't seen this type of a story or thought of it as a creative possibility." To assist the imagination, Room to Read leads workshops to train locals to be children's book authors and illustrators. Berger illustrates concepts of visual storytelling— using details in the illustrations to tell a more complex story, even if the text is very simple. Results vary across countries. In parts of Africa, artists typically have less professional training and fewer resources at their disposal. "The work may be painted with student watercolors on newsprint, scanned in at the local copy shop," Berger notes. At the other end, Room to Read's team in Vietnam is particularly strong. "We work with some incredibly talented, very young and eager folks raised on anime and fun cartoony sort of child-appealing artwork, with visual vocabularies. They are fantastic and have really been able to do some work that has attracted the eye of Vietnamese publishing."

Pratham Books

While publishing is a side endeavor for Room to Read, it is the core mission of Pratham Books, a charity based in India. In 1995, the Indian educational organization Pratham began providing early education to children in the slums of Mumbai. Today, Pratham is the country's largest nongovernmental educational organization, serving 4.7 million children throughout India through a network of tens of thousands of volunteers. Pratham's mission focuses on eradicating illiteracy in order to break the cycle of poverty, under the slogan "Every child in school and learning well."

The scale of this challenge is enormous: an estimated 40 percent of the world's illiterate children live in India. Suzanne Singh, chairwoman of Pratham Books, explains: "Half of children with three years of school cannot read on [their grade] level. Because they cannot read, they cannot learn, and in a few years the dropouts begin." Ultimately, about half of Indian children drop out of school, unless interventions to improve reading succeed. Recognizing this, Pratham has piloted, tested, and scaled up cost-effective educational interventions that rapidly improve child literacy.

As these efforts began to achieve success, Pratham recognized the need to support emerging skills with more reading material. "So libraries began to get set up," Singh recounts. "And as Pratham set up these libraries, they realized there was not enough content available in many languages. Not enough content for sale, and not at realistic price points." Pratham spoke to commercial publishers in India and asked them to develop a special line of books that would meet the organization's needs, but did not get a sufficiently enthusiastic response. Rather than give up, three entrepreneurial philanthropists—Rohini Nilekani, Ashok Kamatha, and Rekha Menon—decided to publish the needed books themselves. In this way, Pratham Books was born.

From the start, Pratham Books was organized as a distinct organization from Pratham. Pratham Books is an independent social enterprise with its own executive board, although it remains in close communication with the older and larger organization. Rohini Nilekani, the founding chairperson of Pratham Books, described its ambitious mission: "We would enable appropriate, indigenous content of high quality and an attractive price, and in multiple languages, to democratize the joy of reading for India's children." At the beginning, Nilekani admits, "We had more passion than experience. We had more commitment than competence." Through experimentation and error, however, the startup found its way. Today,

Pratham Books is a global leader in charitable publishing innovation.

Nilekani herself penned one of the first titles, *The Annual Haircut Day*, using the pseudonym Noni. Nilekani's delightful book tells the story of a village man with very long hair who wants to have it cut. Unfortunately, everyone is too busy cutting the hair of other people. This problem ultimately leads him to a dramatic encounter with a tiger and a satisfying conclusion. The story derives much of its charm from a classic device of children's literature: exaggerated repetition of a silly-sounding phrase. In this case, the silly phrase is the name of the primary character, Sringeri Srinivas. Because the phrase is a name, it appears identically in all translations of the book—currently including English, Hindi, Kannada, Marathi, Telugu, Tamil, Urdu, Gujarati, Punjabi, Bengali, Oriya, Assamese, and Malayalam. Silly Sringeri Srinivas went on to star in other Pratham Books titles, including *Too Many Bananas* and *Too Much Noise*.

In the first year, most copies went to Pratham educators, as originally anticipated. By the second or third year, Singh notes with pride, "everyone was buying from us." Today, around 15 percent of Pratham Books' production goes into the Pratham network. Other major institutional buyers include Room to Read, UNICEF, the Akshara

Foundation, and the Swades Foundation, as well as many smaller ones. According to Singh, "Anybody who is working in the space of literacy for children buys our books." Many schools also use local funds to purchase Pratham Books titles featured on the recommended reading lists of India's Central Board of Secondary Education. Pratham Books now has more than 11 million copies in circulation, mostly in schools and other institutions where they can be used by many children. Through statistical sampling methodology, Pratham Books has estimated that its titles have been read at least 52 million times.

Pratham Books initially relied on members of its staff and network of teachers and volunteers to write and illustrate its first dozen or two stories. Very early on, however, Pratham Books began to commission titles by drawing on the same roster of professional authors and illustrators used by commercial publishers in India. In this way, Pratham Books reproduced a tried-and-true publishing business model. The twist is that philanthropy covers the cost of book development, and the sales price covers only the marginal costs of paper, printing, and distribution. This straightforward approach to creating local literature has worked well in India. The genre of illustrated children's storybooks is already familiar to India's English-fluent middle class. There is also a deep roster of local artistic talent to draw upon, including professional illustrators working in animation and marketing.

Pratham Books has also used a workshop approach, similar to Room to Read's, for some titles. Manisha Chaudhry describes a particularly successful workshop in an extremely challenging setting. "Odisha has over 62 tribes," Chaudhry explains. "These tribes live very close to nature and have a great oral literature. But these students are really at a disadvantage, because there is no printed material available in their language." Pratham Books editor Mala Kumar picks up the story: "We went there with the partner organization that has worked there for a long time, where we listened to stories we had never heard." Chaudhry continues: "We stayed together for three days with eighteen authors from four of these languages. We explored the idea of why a book, why is it important to write a book, why for children? After that they started writing, because they have a lot of stories. But they are used to storytelling, adding details with their eye movement or their hand movement. We needed to stress that you need to be descriptive in the book because the child cannot see your eye movement or hand movement." More than fifty finished stories were read to children from the community to select the ten most popular. Artists in the local tradition of mural painting were recruited for an illustrators' workshop. "The books came out brilliant," Chaudhry beams. "That style of illustration was new to every other person in the country, and it had a modern twist. And the stories were so cute."

Use of translation to accommodate linguistic diversity was central from the beginning. Manisha Chaudhry, head of content development for Pratham Books, explains the challenge. "There are 786 languages spoken in India on last count. About 29 are officially recognized languages by the government of India. But there are several more that have scripts, and even without government support are producing literature." Chaudhry explains how the organization chose which languages to prioritize. "We started out with English, Hindi, Marathi, and Kannada in 2004. English is international and spoken by all of us, being an ex-colony of the British. If you are a middle-class Indian, you are most likely to be educated in an English-medium school." Other languages were more idiosyncratically prioritized. Pratham began in the city of Mumbai, serving largely Marathi-speaking children. Kannada is the official state language of the nearby city of Bangalore, where Pratham Books is headquartered. Over time, Pratham Books added more Indian languages, and now publishes in more than twenty. A single title is typically printed in at least a dozen languages.

Once all translations are prepared and triple-checked for accuracy, the entire batch goes to printing. By ordering very large print runs across multiple languages, Pratham Books secures better prices. Printers realize economies of scale when they fulfill such orders, because the illustration plates are the same across all the languages, and only the black plate containing the text must be changed. Much of the savings is passed along. Chaudhry explains, "We don't go in for printing until it's ready in at least 6 languages—that is the only way we can leverage economies of scale. Our first print run is usually 8,000–10,000 copies. English and Hindi would be larger, and some of the other languages would be smaller, but nothing less than 500 copies."

Working in non-Roman scripts brings special challenges. "The digital fonts are very well developed in English, but in Indic languages the fonts have a tendency to break up when it goes into printing," Chaudhry explains. "So it is proofed again and again and again and there is lots of loss in transfer. So if you upload a book in Delhi for printing here, there is every chance that there might be a loss of a diacritic, and if that critical little mark drops off it may change the word and even the meaning of the story. So the proofing has to be very sharp." Pratham Books' lead editor, Mala Kumar, agrees: "Our gestation periods are really long, considering that many of our books are only 12 pages long, 8 pages plus a cover. But multiplied into ten languages, with these problems in each of the languages, the production and proofing necessarily takes a very long time."

To support this work, Pratham Books prioritizes hiring staff members with multiple language competencies. Chaudhry, for instance, can write both in English and in Hindi, her mother tongue. She also understands Punjabi and Bangla. Mala Kumar writes in English, Hindi, and Tamil, and can understand Kannada and a bit of Gujarati. Kumar explains, "Even though I may not have the language expertise needed to write or review or edit a book in that language, I would be able to talk to people doing that in that language to find out if they are competent enough in that language. I would be talking to people in the southern states who become our resource people there. Similarly, the other editors also get their people around the state they live in, so we get the most authentic voices reflecting that language and local culture. It is still a challenge because there are so many ways of speaking a language."

The Right to Read

A connection between reading and human rights has long been recognized in terms of liberty from censorship. In the 1960s, the global community dedicated increased attention to the entitlement of education for literacy. Today, the critical connection between reading and human rights is the need to expand the availability of reading material. Too few children have access to the books they need to develop as readers, particularly in disadvantaged languages. Supporting the right to read means believing that reading for education and pleasure is the entitlement of every child, rather than a privilege of those born into certain language communities.

The right to read is not a new human right, but simply a new way of looking at older ones. Since 1948, international human rights documents have recognized several closely related human rights: freedom of expression, the right to education, the right to science and culture, and minority cultural rights. Between 1989 and today, nearly every country in the world has also joined the newer United Nations Convention on the Rights of the Child. Article 17 of this convention establishes each government's duty to ensure every child can access media that supports his or her physical, mental, social, moral, and spiritual well-being. It also specifically commits national governments to "encourage the production and distribution of children's books," particularly in minority and indigenous languages and through international cooperation.

Many organizations are working to expand multilingual children's literature: the African Storybook Project, Books for Asia, the Global Book Alliance, Nabu.org, Worldreader, and myriad small publishers serving specific language communities. Room to Read and Pratham Books are two of the largest and most successful. Their programs make clearer than ever before what it means to effectively promote the right to read. These efforts must be multiplied many times over, in every country and for every language. A task of this scale is not one that any single charity, or even a handful of international agencies, can accomplish on its own. It will require the coordinated efforts of the United Nations, national governments, foundations, businesspeople, charities, publishers, authors, and illustrators. Recognition of the universal human right to read offers a moral framework to unite their efforts.

FIVE

Reinventing Distribution

John Wood was inspired to found Room to Read while backpacking through Nepal. Residents of a mountain village impressed Wood with their eagerness to read, but lack of resources. After returning to the United States, Wood asked family and friends to mail book donations to his home, at their own expense. From there, Wood and his father packed them up in suitcases and boxes to take as baggage on their international flight. Once on the ground in Nepal, both passengers and cargo traveled by truck to the base of the mountain. From there, yak drivers actually loaded the books onto the animals' backs to ascend the steep paths. Yak-back transportation may be unique to Nepal, but the need for innovative methods of moving books to where they are needed is universal.

During my research, I asked nearly everyone which they have found to be more difficult: Creating wonderful new books that meet the needs of all readers? Or solving the logistical challenge of how to get those books into the hands of all the people who need them? It was not a close contest. Respondents were unanimous that distribution is harder. Developing countries especially contend with limited transportation infrastructure and unreliable postal systems.

Even in the United States, however, the "last mile" challenge is enormous. Erica Perl, vice president of First Book, encapsulates her organization's concern for distribution. "Even though there are books that aren't being written, I do feel like there is still a huge issue with that. There are great books that aren't getting to the readers." First Book's president Kyle Zimmer adds, "We are deliriously happy to reach 164,000 groups. But at the same time, we have to remember that what we reach is perhaps 10 percent or 12 percent of the kids who need us. We are such a long way from cracking it open."

Melody Zavala of Books for Asia echoes this view. "I think the last mile is always the most difficult in any program; making sure that the books really reach the most disadvantaged people who most need them." In addition to cost and language barriers, geographic barriers cut many communities off from books. Zavala continues, "Having that reach all the way out to far-flung communities that don't have all of this infrastructure, being able to really reach a product that far is definitely the most difficult part." Imagination Library confronts the same challenge when serving rural and Native communities in North America. "There's a lot of empty space in Canada," David Dotson points out. "We don't take that infrastructure for granted." For readers isolated by snow and simple extreme distance, books must come in by plane.

From Pratham Books' perspective, "Creating access is infinitely harder than creating books," Suzanne Singh states unequivocally. "Getting books into the last village in the last state that is very underserved is really, really hard. We have constantly had to innovate and do really radical stuff." Singh describes some of the creative approaches her organization has tried. "We have worked with the postal system, since that is available in every little village: can they be the carriers of our books? And there are companies that sell soaps and detergent. We partnered with them to load books onto their trucks. Solar companies that sell lights and cookers in underserved areas." None of these methods proved satisfactory.

"Creating access to reach the underserved child is probably the biggest and most challenging thing that we've done."

Books for Asia

Not far from the Oakland port on the San Francisco Bay, four or five staff members occupy offices at the front of a large warehouse. This is the global headquarters of Books for Asia. At the front of Books for Asia's California warehouse, large bay doors slide up to allow trucks twenty to forty feet long to offload pallets stacked high with books donated by U.S. publishers. The floor is dotted with twenty or so large pallets, each stacked with simple but colorful paperbacks. The back portion of the warehouse resembles the self-service section of an IKEA store. Towering shelves support boxes upon boxes of books that will move more slowly: overstocked medical textbooks, dictionaries, and academic titles that underperformed the publishers' hopes for crossover appeal. A typical book might spend three to six months in this warehouse before shipping out.

Along several rows of folding tables, two young women pick books from various piles to complete a specific packing list. Each box is destined for a particular country. Today, the team is at work preparing a forty-foot shipping container destined for Myanmar. Later this month they will send shipments to Vietnam and Pakistan. The deliveries are carefully planned to use the space of a standard shipping container as efficiently as possible. Once overseas, some of these containers will be loaded onto trucks, others on railroad cars. Each will ultimately find its way to overseas schools, universities, and community organizations. "Fortunately we have an Asia Foundation office and staff with great networks in just about every country where we distribute books," Zavala notes. The Asia Foundation has negotiated duty-free arrangements with each government, so that no taxes are imposed on the entry of Books for Asia containers.

The Books for Asia program works similarly to food-rescue organizations, which distribute donations of unsold food items to charitable pantries across a city. The U.S. publishing industry operates on consignment, meaning that booksellers can generally return books they are unable to sell to the publisher. If too many books are returned, the publisher has to find ways to dispose of them. This has long meant that publishers are eager to collaborate with book charities by donating remaindered copies. Wendy Rocket, Books for Asia's communications director, explains: "With our book donations from American publishers, because we have been doing this for a while, we are able to get the volume needed to achieve economies of scale." Their stock is generally in English, but they are sought after by universities and lower schools where English is the second language. "Because we have this access to this particular supply of books, we are able to meet a very specific, and from what we are told, a still very relevant demand in Asia." Ironically, a book may be printed in Singapore, then travel through California and Ohio to end up on a book shelf in New York City; later, it returns through Ohio and California to find its way back to Singapore.

"We talk about our work sometimes as matchmaking," Rocket explains. "We see what books our publishers have to donate, and we have a system of choosing and collecting. And then we coordinate with our staff in Asia." This work is vital to ensure that books end up in places where they will actually be useful. Some countries have significant need for medical textbooks, while others cannot use them. A nursing college in Vietnam might report that it particularly needs drug reference handbooks. Books about Christmas will delight children in the Philippines but not in Afghanistan. India cannot accept any books with maps that "misrepresent" its disputed Kashmiri border with Pakistan. And every partner has a limit on the number of copies of any one title that it can usefully distribute.

Although the books are donated by publishers at no cost, "shipping and handling" expenses are significant. Books for Asia does the work of unloading, sorting, storing, matchmaking, planning, packing, and sending. It can take anywhere from two to six weeks to process a large donation from a publisher. Correctly labeled boxes full of the same book are easiest to sort and stack. Many boxes, however, come with a hodgepodge of remaindered books returned by a single bookstore. These must be individually catalogued and stacked on shelves. Staff time is needed for cultivating publisher partnerships, managing the warehouse, coordinating with overseas partners, and planning shipments. Increasingly, U.S. publishers expect the charity to pick up the cost of transporting donated books from their midwestern hubs to the Bay Area. In recent years, the organization has gone from shipping approximately a million books per year to less than half that number, because of budgetary pressure. The funds simply are not there to move the books.

On the other side of the ocean, local partners must manage a similarly challenging set of logistics. Melody Zavala, also of Books for Asia, explains: "There is a whole variety of distribution methods at that point. In many places, there are always people coming to the capital city for some reason. In some places, it is easy enough and cheap enough to send it through the postal system or by truck or by boat. In another place, all the school principals come to the capital for their annual meeting with the ministry, and they are empowered to do the pickup. There is an incredible variety of ways, sometimes going out with other Asia Foundation programs. In Vietnam, the national library of Vietnam has big and tiny libraries across the country, all the way down to village level, and they take on the distribution."

Supply Chain Innovation

Whether commercial or charitable, distribution at large scale requires sophisticated logistics. There are a million ways to move books, but not all approaches are equally efficient. Dedicated brick-and-mortar bookstores are incredibly expensive. Amazon.com disrupted this market by cutting costs in the supply chain through innovations such as online shopping, the Amazon.com second-hand marketplace, regional fulfillment centers, Kindles, and e-books. To reach even a fraction of the global population hungry for books, similarly radical supply-chain innovations are needed. First Book and Imagination Library—both introduced in Chapter 2—have been particularly successful in driving down the cost of delivery in order to expand the population they can serve.

First Book's earliest distribution model, the National Book Bank, took a very businesslike approach to squeezing every drop of value out of a transaction. The charity found it could take advantage of donated warehouse space to temporarily hold large volumes of remaindered books. First Book emailed its literacy partners on a monthly or biweekly basis to let them know what titles were in stock. A national network of volunteers handled packaging, loading, and delivery of the resulting orders. These cost-cutting measures helped First Book drive costs down to fifty-five to seventy-five cents per book, while offering teachers the ability to choose specific titles in bulk.

Today, First Book's literacy partners can also shop online. In this newer delivery model, First Book purchases books from publishers at a discount. Paying for books, rather than waiting for donations, makes the model highly scalable. First Book now processes more purchased books than donated ones. Each order is mailed via UPS at discounted rates. Partners may order any number of copies, with free shipping on orders of twenty-five dollars or more. The challenge to scale lies at the periphery of the distribution network. Literacy organizations and classrooms are the crucial final link in the supply chain. To fully leverage this link, First Book launched a national marketing campaign to make teachers aware of the service.

Imagination Library approaches the last-mile problem in a different way, by mailing books directly to children's homes. Publishers specially print the books to order and ship them to Imagination Library's hub in Knoxville, Tennessee. From there, distribution to each participating community is handled by Direct Mail Services, a family-owned business that has worked with Imagination Library from the very beginning. This shipping method takes advantage of bulk mail rates offered by the United States Postal Service, more commonly used by magazines and shopping catalogs. Tall stacks of paperback books are delivered to postal distribution centers in low-income neighborhoods. Mail carriers distribute books to the designated addresses along with other mail. Print runs are calculated to cover exactly the number of copies to be delivered, without warehousing.

"We spend cents on shipment here in the U.S.," Dotson says. Cost-effective distribution has allowed the organization to expand greatly. Imagination Library currently reaches 4 percent of all children up to five years old in the United States. Dotson hopes this will soon reach 10 percent of the target age group. "This would be bigger than WIC, bigger than Head Start," Dotson explains. "Things that you think are giant, 10 percent would dwarf that."

Imagination Library already operates in Canada, England, and Australia, Dotson notes, meaning that the program "will soon exhaust the supply of English-speaking countries with postal systems." Imagination Library would like to work in more countries, but this will require further supply-chain innovation. A pilot program in Belize ships books from the U.S. every three months to achieve the necessary volume, hand-delivering them monthly through a network of local churches. The goal is to work at scale in several more countries by 2020. Latin America is the obvious first target, because Spanish is used throughout the region.

So far, no organization has attempted Imagination Library's direct-to-the-child delivery model in a multilingual context. Theoretically, it could be quite efficient. Parents already give their child's age and address at signup; they could also list a language preference. Local networks could be leveraged to sign up a critical mass of families speaking a certain language. At least in neighborhoods with a high concentration of families speaking a certain language, the economics should work out. The approach should work well for Spanish-speaking families in the United States, or Arabic-speaking families in France and Germany. For developing countries with an underdeveloped postal system and intense linguistic diversity, the challenges are even greater.

The Limits of Print Distribution

Pratham Books sells around one million print copies of its books to major charities and schools each year. Figuring out how to grow outside of these institutional channels has been more challenging. Purvi Shah came from a background in marketing and distribution. Since joining Pratham Books, she has exhaustively experimented with creative approaches to deliver books to villages across India. The challenge is extraordinarily complicated.

"Say for argument's sake we ride a Coca-Cola distribution network," Shah suggests, imagining a corporate partnership to ship books alongside crates of Coke. "Theirs is probably the deepest and farthest in India. But I do not know what languages they need in which villages, and the level of the child there." Books present a complex distribution challenge. Anyone can enjoy a Coke. The same product can be shipped to anywhere in the world. Soap, sugar, gasoline, matches, and even vaccinations work similarly. Pratham Books has more than two thousand different products, however: hundreds of titles in dozens of languages at varying reading levels. And this is just for children in primary schools. Teenagers and adults have even more individualized information needs and genre preferences. For books to be useful, it is essential that each reader is matched with the appropriate product.

With physical distribution, Shah realized, "We could never get that match out." This insight has pushed Pratham Books to emphasize digital distribution in its strategic planning. Shah has moved from working on corporate distribution partnerships to heading Digital Projects. Through the Internet, any school in any community can locate books in the right language, at the right level, on a particular theme of interest. The desired title can then be promptly delivered anywhere in the country, with zero shipping and handling costs. For communities without reliable Internet service, hundreds of digital books can fit onto a tiny memory card, traveling easily in a pocket or bag.

Where postal systems are strong, they offer a convenient and cost-effective way to deliver hard-copy books. In the United States, Imagination Library spends pennies per book to ship directly to children's homes. The trade-off, however, is that the recipients have no ability to select particular books of interest. The distributional economies of scale depend on sending the same book at the same time to every child in a particular zip code. To provide greater inventory and choice, First Book manages an even more sophisticated distribution system, mimicking that of online book retailers. In this model, distribution costs around one dollar per book.

These methods are more challenging to deploy in developing countries, because of greater geographic barriers, underdeveloped infrastructure, and unreliable postal systems. "That kind of distribution system is not set up in these places," explains Susan Rimerman of Worldreader. "When a publisher came from South Africa to our summit in Kenya, they brought two huge suitcases of books. That was part of their distribution method!" Because Books for Asia serves overseas readers, its distribution costs are higher, around $2.50 per book. That investment pays off handsomely for a medical textbook that retails for more than $100. The value proposition is much less compelling for children's paperbacks, though country partners are desperate for these much-needed materials. Rimerman points out: "In the U.S., you can order books from Amazon and have them on your doorstep in three days. They just magically appear. People don't think about the infrastructure that made that happen."

Digital technology offers to make books "magically appear" in a different way. When an e-book is requested, you do not need to pay an employee to check whether it is in stock, find it on the shelf, and pack it. You do not need to load and insure and ship and unload. You do not need to warehouse a local supply or wait weeks for arrival from halfway around the world. Yes, software still has to be designed, but this can scale to deliver millions of books at less than a penny apiece. The software you need may already exist. For charities looking to make their budgets stretch, these potential cost savings are significant and very attractive. For this reason, literacy charities in the developing world are increasingly emphasizing digital content.

SIX

Going Digital

When Apple personal computers were first introduced for home use in 1984, the 128-kilobyte unit cost nearly $6,000 in today's dollars. Thirty-five years later, portable Chromebooks with a full color screen, Internet capability, and vastly greater processing power start at around $150. I recently bought a touch-screen tablet for $35. By the time you read this, that may seem high. Since the 1960s, computer power has doubled about every two years. This phenomenon has been so steady and predictable that it has come to be referred to as Moore's Law. A corollary is that digital devices are steadily becoming more and more affordable.

A digital divide still exists between rich and poor, but it's smaller than you might think. According to a study by

Victoria Rideout and Vikki Katz published in 2016, more than 90 percent of American families living below the poverty line have access to the Internet; 85 percent have some kind of mobile device, and 69 percent have some type of computer. The quality of access still varies greatly between rich and poor. Lower-income families tend to have slower connections, limited data plans, and fewer devices. The basic components, however, have already become affordable to nearly everyone in the United States.

Even in the developing world, Internet-capable technologies are rapidly becoming universal. Here also, mobile phones lead the way. Nokia's most basic feature phone—with a small color screen, alphanumeric keypad, flash camera, mobile, wifi, and Bluetooth capabilities—is available for just U.S. $25 in Kenya. A Tecno Spark smartphone—with full-sized screen, digital camera, and fingerprint sensor—sells for around $85. By 2020, smartphone adoption is expected to reach 55 percent in sub-Saharan Africa, 63 percent in Asia, 64 percent in the Arab world, and 70 percent in Latin America. The number of people using mobile phones and tablets to access the Internet doubled between 2012 and 2017; the mobile phone industry trade association known as GSMA expects that figure to reach 4.7 billion by 2020. The high rate of mobile access, even among the poor, opens tremendous new opportunities to address book hunger through digital distribution models.

African Storybook Project

In a Tanzanian library, more than a hundred children sit cross-legged on the floor. They have come on a field trip from a nearby school. The librarian, recently trained in the operation of a two-hundred-dollar laptop and a three-hundred-dollar projector, displays an African Storybook Project digital story onto a sheet at the front of the room. The gathered children are as excited by this new media experience as American kids would be at an IMAX theater. The librarian reads each line of text, then has the children repeat it back as a group. The story is locally relevant and entertaining. The children are fully engaged; some of them are literally rolling on the floor with laughter. In one month, fourteen thousand schoolchildren will make twenty-three thousand visits to this library. If visits continue at this rate for a year, the cost approaches something on the order of a penny per child.

Africa will strike some as an unlikely setting for cutting-edge, high-tech approaches. It has the lowest rate of Internet access of any continent, and familiarity with computers is limited even among teachers and librarians.

Technology that may be affordable by American standards remains costly relative to African incomes. Moreover, prices for the same technology are often substantially higher in developing countries, because of import taxes and distribution difficulties. An iPad in Kenya, for example, might cost twice as much as one purchased from a U.S. discount store. Many communities still have unreliable electricity sources.

These challenges, however, are actually less intimidating than the challenges of distributing printed books across land. The continent is vast, and much of it is landlocked, without access to seaports except through a neighboring country. Railways and highway systems are underdeveloped, and most of the population still lives in rural areas. Corruption and theft result in significant losses along the textbook supply chain, and postal services are similarly unreliable. In comparison, the challenges of digital distribution are quite manageable.

The African Storybook Project formats the books it creates as digital slide shows. This allows them to be opened on standard-issue software, such as Microsoft PowerPoint or any of the free alternatives. These can be digitally projected for reading in a large group. Even a smartphone screen can be made large enough for a small group of students to read through a cheap plastic magnifier. African Storybook Project is also experimenting with on-demand printing technologies to avoid distribution hurdles typically associated with print books. ASP's Tessa Welch explains: "I think it is important for children to have books in their hands, but maybe not distributed so far. Maybe if the library has a printer, a child can take home a particular book on loan."

A Library in Every Pocket

After working as a Microsoft executive and overseeing sales at Amazon, David Risher spent a year traveling the world with his wife and two young daughters. Near the end of the trip, his family was visiting an orphanage when Risher noticed a padlocked building. It was the library. Risher, a book lover and comparative literature major, asked to look inside. The orphanage director confessed that she did not know where to find the key. Like many small libraries in the developing world, it had simply fallen into disuse. Its collection of discarded American books held little interest or relevance for local children with limited English. It might as well have been a long-distance landfill.

"That was it, that was my moment," Risher says. "I looked through my life and I saw books over and over again and technology over and over again." Risher came back to San Francisco and founded Worldreader as a charitable startup. He estimates at least a billion people are held back by low literacy and book hunger. To Risher, this is not just a tragedy; it is a business opportunity. "Ours is a social enterprise, but we still think of it as a business." In starting any business, Risher explains, "you want to make sure you're solving a real problem, and you want to make sure you're trying to do it in a way that's different from what people have tried before." Delivering relevant books to readers in the developing world was clearly a big problem. Given his background, Risher naturally saw the potential to solve this problem digitally.

In the basement of Worldreader's San Francisco office, a technology team loads the library onto devices for a school in Kenya. Dozens of wires dangle from an Ikea shelf. Each Kindle must rest here for two hours to receive its library. The Kindles cost thirty dollars each, thanks to a discount from Amazon. Fully loaded, the pocket library of one hundred titles costs around seventy dollars. A hand-drawn diagram calculates how long each step in the process takes, which determines how many Kindles can be loaded in a day. The goal is eventually to shift this process to the country where the Kindles are used. This will create jobs abroad, save on labor costs, and, most important, cut down the lead time to set up a new school.

For the moment, loaded Kindles get packed into cardboard boxes to be shipped overseas.

The work doesn't end once the boxes reach their destination. Worldreader also works to train the teachers on the technology, literacy methods, and gender sensitivity. Female students in Ghana, for instance, typically lag far behind their male peers. In Worldreader schools, the gender achievement gap disappears. The program even includes training on how to conduct local fundraising to ensure the school can buy additional e-books in the future—an added bonus for schools and for local publishers. In communities without electricity, solar panels will be installed at the school. The long battery life of the dedicated e-reader means that students can charge the device at school and still take it home to share with siblings and parents.

Ensuring the sustainable production of locally relevant content is also a goal. Staff members think in terms of cultivating an entire digital ecosystem around local books. Worldreader works with local publishers to digitize their books for the first time, and trains them on how to market their e-books at Amazon.com for global sales. "Even though there are only a small number of new books published in Africa each year, if we can unlock their backlist of books and digitize them, we have got an incredible resource," Risher says. American publishers donate content, while African publishers are paid about seventy cents (U.S.) per e-book. This can add up to a regular stream of several thousand dollars per year for a small publisher. From these resources, a customized library of around one hundred books is created for each school.

Risher brings a mindset shaped by his years managing Amazon's explosive growth. Worldreader now operates on a $10 million annual budget—this includes the value of donated e-books—and has already reached more than five million readers. It is still in the stage of refining its programs and optimizing its model, with an eye toward much greater expansion over the next decade. Worldreader hopes to serve forty million readers by 2020, and one billion by 2025.

Although both print books and dedicated e-readers have their place, the cheapest strategy by far is to deliver e-books to devices people already own. Library for All, now Nabu.org, has prioritized this approach from the beginning. Its cofounder Tanyella Evans explains: "Our [mobile] distribution strategy is really driven by the market—these Chinese and Asian companies producing these low-cost handsets. People know what *Tecno* and *Blu* are, even in these rural areas. It's like Coca-Cola." Unlike Worldreader's Kindle strategy, "we believed that the potential was in the device-agnostic platform." Smart-phones also made it possible to distribute illustrations in color, which was important to Library for All's vision of a high-quality digital reading experience.

Worldreader has since deployed a cell-phone strategy as a complement to its longer-standing Kindle programs. Whereas Worldreader's Kindle programs focus on school-based instruction, its mobile programs target out-of-school adults and preschoolers. Its mobile platform got an early boost from a partnership with Opera, which at that time held 25 percent of the mobile phone browser market. In this partnership, the Worldreader app came preinstalled on most phones distributed in the developing world, greatly boosting its visibility. Mobile delivery "allows us to move quickly," Susan Rimerman of Worldreader points out. "People already have the device. We have huge audiences in Ethiopia, Nigeria, and the Philippines. We can put books in people's hands where we don't have the resources to put feet on the ground." This enables Worldreader to expand nimbly into new languages or settings.

Whether on a mobile phone or dedicated e-reader, the digital strategy "is absolutely tied to our success," Rimer-man notes. "We now have books in 43 languages and it enables us to quickly add depth to our collection. The cost to prepare smaller print runs for small language groups makes it expensive—we jump over that hurdle." After discovering that romance was a hot category among women in Muslim areas of Nigeria, for example, Worldreader was able to quickly load more Harlequin titles. This agility also came in handy when the organization obtained funding to launch an Arabic-language program with Syrian refugees in Jordan. "One of the great things about digital is that you don't have the limits of print and paper or the logistical challenges of distribution beyond your local market," Rimerman notes. "You can just get your books out there."

Digital Versus Print?

The rise of e-readers sparked significant controversy among U.S. book lovers. Can reading on a screen really be "as good" as reading on paper? American bibliophiles tend to have strong opinions one way or another. Supporters praise the convenience of instant access and portability. Detractors say the devices rob readers of the tactile coziness of holding a book in one's hands, turning the pages, feeling and smelling the paper.

Recently, it seems that the detractors are winning, at least in the United States. Sales of e-books peaked at 36 percent of the U.S. book market in 2014, but are now declining. According to the Codex Group, the primary reason is "digital fatigue." Americans spend too much time on their screens already. For print media, they are happy to seize the option to read on paper. Indeed, digital natives are leading the way in fleeing e-books for print. Americans also have high standards for digital reading, and strongly prefer reading on a Kindle, Nook, or tablet. Cell phone purchases are only 3 percent of all e-book sales in the United States. Of course, American readers need only wait a day or two for Amazon to deliver a print book to their doorstep. Paper remains a very convenient, and perhaps the most pleasant, way to read for American book buyers.

Readers experiencing book hunger, however, are less picky about their options. According to Rimerman: "People in North America and Europe are really hung up on paper versus digital. When you talk to African librarians, they don't care. They don't have this attachment to paper. They say, 'We're fine, we just want the books.' " For many low-income readers in Africa and elsewhere, print books remain hopelessly out of reach. To encounter a digital library on one's cell phone is to experience the same awe and excitement that American book lovers might feel walking into a particularly outstanding book store. For readers who have never owned a laptop or a tablet, a tiny smartphone screen feels miraculous rather than inferior.

Most book nonprofits currently taking advantage of digital distribution possibilities are using common e-book formats such as ePub and PDF. Some publishers, however, are experimenting with more creative formats. Instead of attempting to recreate the experience of a paper book on a digital device, these "digital first" strategies reimagine the book to leverage the capabilities of digital devices. Rather than adopt the e-book formats common in the United States, Pratham Books formats stories in a way that is optimized for reading on mobile phones. Readers scroll down through text interspersed with pictures, without ever turning a page. The format imitates the layout of web pages, which were themselves designed for digital reading, rather than the traditional layout of paper binding. As software to support mobile reading has advanced, nonprofit publishers no longer have to create their own distribution platforms.

It would be a mistake, however, to think of mobile reading as a complete substitute for print. "For children's books, when a picture book is laid out with big illustrations, and the text is designed beautifully on top of that image, it's a great reading experience," Rimerman acknowledges. Digital devices are not yet there. Even when mobile capability does become nearly universal, traditional paper books will probably continue to play an important role for novice readers. Worldreader has found that teachers who had previously used paper books find it easier to adjust to using Kindles. In contrast, first-grade students often have difficulty operating a Kindle even after months of practice. Print on paper is more accessible for novice readers—assuming they can get their hands on such books. "Digital is not going to be right in every scenario," acknowledges Evans; "this is not a silver-bullet solution. We want to make sure the content we are creating is print-ready so that is an option."

Melody Zavala of Books for Asia agrees. For decades, the organization has focused on distributing physical books donated by U.S. publishers. More recently, Books for Asia has seized on digital distribution as a way to meet critical needs for mother-tongue content. "It is amazing, digital access and the use of mobile phones, where we are it is huge, it is skyrocketing. It is important to program for that and take advantage of that—but also to know that in some places, the barriers are so huge that it's not going to happen. We need a variety of approaches. The world is a complicated place. For anyone to say that digital is the solution, or that it has to be all print . . . there is no flipping of the switch here. The mix is important. We're going to continue to do that mix for a long time."

The Digital Advantage

As hardware and software efficiencies continue to improve, so do the advantages of digital distribution. Paper, trucks, and warehouses are expensive, particularly for a large-scale operation. Of course, mobile phones, software, and Internet connections also cost money. But where readers have already acquired these for basic communication, e-book distribution can "free-ride" on the existing system. Physical distribution barriers rooted in long distances, mountainous terrain, poor infrastructure, corruption, and limited logistical expertise become irrelevant.

Digital distribution also brings cost advantages to content development. Major publishers find it simple and nearly costless to donate e-books. "At first it makes them nervous that they are going to turn titles over in digital format for mobile availability," Rimerman acknowledges. "Piracy is a concern for some publishers." Systems have been designed, however, to make it virtually impossible to download whole books. In contrast, for-profit publishers cannot afford to print paper books for the sole purpose of donating them to charity. Even with a tax credit, doing this would result in a financial loss. Instead, publishers donate paper books only when they have miscalculated demand and printed more copies than they were able to sell. Even then, charities must cover the costs of collecting the remaindered copies and distributing them to readers.

The digital revolution also enhances prospects for diverse books. In a print world, titles with niche appeal are risky to invest in. They cost much more to produce per copy, because editing, design, and even printing all depend on economies of scale. Niche books cannot be stocked in a brick-and-mortar bookstore, where the hypothetical reader interested in a particular title may simply never come along. The rise of online booksellers and digital publishing has led to an explosion in titles available in the United States, precisely because these constraints no longer apply. A corollary of greater affordability is that a title does not have to be a best-seller in order to be financially viable. Older titles now out of print remain available.

Closely related to this point is the advantage of digital distribution for accommodating linguistic diversity. According to Evans: "In Uganda there are 52 different languages. To print all the different versions of those books, no one would want to invest in that as a print strategy. Reversioning is only cost-effective digitally." A neighborhood bookshop might carry a few dozen titles, and an urban bookstore several hundred titles. But mobile devices connected to a cloud library can offer access to millions of different titles. This is crucial in multilingual contexts, where the population of a single city may need access to books in hundreds of languages. This complexity of offerings could never be accomplished in print distribution. Traditional publishers and bookstores by necessity specialize in one or two languages. In the digital world, hundreds of thousands of books are quickly searchable by language, reading level, and topic.

Digital technologies also make it easier to pay for publishing. Once a title is made available, a digital copy can be transported to a reader anywhere in the world for pennies on the dollar. This has two implications. First, nonprofits can have a much greater impact with their charitable dollars. Second, and perhaps more transformatively, it may become possible to charge developing-world readers, schools, or libraries highly affordable prices— perhaps a nickel or a dime per e-book. Even this very low income might support a financially self-sustaining model that would enable much faster growth. Smartphone and platform companies also have a business interest in supporting charitable publishing. Free libraries represent yet another value-adding feature that can motivate consumers to purchase a smartphone, or to spend more time on a social platform.

As technology costs continue to drop, the advantages of digital approaches become even more salient. Sooner or later, as with every other sector, digital disruption is coming to charitable book publishing.

SEVEN

Negotiating Permissions

In 1985, George Kerscher left his first career, as a high school teacher of literature, to pursue a graduate degree in computer science at the University of Montana. In addition to the typical challenges of academic study, Kerscher faced a unique one. He had recently lost his vision, and could no longer read normal print. At that time, readers with blindness or low vision could borrow special cassette recordings of many popular novels from national library services. But the specialized texts that Kerscher needed for his studies had never been recorded. Even if they were, it would have been very impractical to navigate assigned pages and reference materials on a cassette tape. At the time, the best solution available was for Kerscher to hire an assistant to personally read the required materials aloud to him.

When Kerscher happened to meet the author of one of his computer science books, however, it occurred to him to ask if the digital file was available. Inspired, he soon wrote to several computer science publishers, requesting files and copyright permission to adapt their books for readers with disabilities. Kerscher spent weeks creating software that would convert the text files into a variety of accessible file formats. Readers requiring large print could easily adjust the font sizes. Those familiar with braille could read the books via a refreshable braille machine, or print a paper copy at home using a special printer. Users of Kurzweil text-to-speech reading machines, first sold in 1976, could listen to an automated audio performance. Realizing that many others like him could benefit from this type of service, Kerscher launched Computerized Books for the Blind and Print Disabled in 1988. "I was trying to reach people who were blind and physically handicapped," Kerscher explains, "but also include people who could not read standard print because of dyslexia or some other learning disability." The enterprise was never formally incorporated as either a for-profit or non-profit organization. "It was just me, in my basement." In those pre-Internet days, Kerscher received book files on floppy disks, and mailed the converted files to other print-disabled readers. "I was shipping all over the world on diskette."

As in many other fields, the introduction of software allowed for a dramatic increase in productivity. Earlier services had to carefully pick and choose their titles, because each audio recording required many hours of volunteer labor to make them accessible. Kerscher's software accomplished this in just five seconds. For the first time, it became practical to convert entire catalogs of printed material into accessible formats. "At Microsoft Press, there was a woman in the publishing department whose father was blind," Kerscher recalls. "Every time they came out with a new book, she would put the book in a box, along with the diskettes, and ship it to me. As soon as I got that box, I processed the files."

Seeking Copyright Permissions

Kerscher's practice of requesting written permission from publishers was not strictly necessary, under *Sony Corporation of America v. Universal City Studios, Inc.*, a Supreme Court decision issued in 1984. Movie and television producers had argued that home users of Betamax, an early VCR technology, were committing copyright infringement by recording programs without their permission.

Sony narrowly won that case, with the Court holding that personal recording for time-shifting purposes was permitted under the fair use doctrine. Another court would almost certainly have applied the same logic to approve format-shifting by a print-disabled reader. Indeed, a footnote in *Sony* recalled that a House committee report had once identified "making a copy of a copyrighted work for the convenience of a blind person" as a prime example of fair use. Kerscher wanted to go further, however, making not just one personal copy but also distributing multiple copies to other print-disabled readers. This too would likely have been deemed fair use, but requesting permission avoided any possibility of dispute. Copyright law aside, Kerscher also needed publishers' assistance to access digital files; in those days, e-books were not yet sold, and scanning technology was still in its infancy.

Requesting copyright permission from publishers was also a well-established practice in the field. Recording for the Blind, an older and larger organization, began its practice of obtaining permission for each title before the Sony precedent was set. Although publishers were generally willing, the process of obtaining copyright permissions was very time consuming. "There were 10 to 20 people employed in this department, establishing the relationships with publishers," Kerscher recalls. "Somebody with the publisher leaves and somebody new comes in, and they are like, 'What do you want this for?' " Not every publisher would respond; those that did typically required multiple follow-up calls. "The copyright license for accessibility is a non-revenue generating activity," Kerscher points out. "If you have two stacks of stuff on your desk and this stack brings in money and this stack does not bring in money, which stack is your boss going to have you work on first?"

Granting copyright permissions can also cost publishers money. Soliciting legal advice on a proposed charitable license can easily cost hundreds of dollars. The lawyer may even recommend an expensive review of each author's contract, to ensure the publisher has the authority to grant the permission. Publishers may also feel obligated to verify that the organization or person contacting them with a request is truly who they say they are. Even dealing with a large, trusted organization takes time and resources. Dealing with many individual requests from smaller organizations is considerably more difficult.

Seeking permission on a title-by-title basis, Kerscher says: "That would have been a show-stopper right there" for a small operation. Recognizing the potential scale his software could enable, Kerscher purposefully requested broader licenses. "I tried to get blanket copyright releases for everything the publisher had." Many publishers obliged. Kerscher only ever worked with around two dozen publishers. That was enough, however, to secure all the books needed for his education in computer science. Thanks in part to the easy availability of accessible learning materials, computer programming became a leading area of employment for men and women with vision impairments.

The Chafee Amendment

In 1996, several national blind advocacy groups collaborated to push forward legislation to ease the laborious process of securing permissions. The bill amended copyright law to clarify that no permission was required from authors or publishers to convert books into accessible formats for print-disabled readers. Recorded as Section 121 of the U.S. Copyright Code, the law is commonly referred to as the Chafee Amendment, in honor of a senator influential to its passage. Organizations serving blind readers gained the ability to include titles without publisher permission. Publishers were also protected against the possibility of suits by authors.

A new nonprofit organization named Benetech emerged to take advantage of this new possibility at greater scale. To advance this work, Jim Fruchterman, founder and CEO, personally developed one of the earliest digital scanners.

Benetech would purchase an ordinary print copy and "chop" the spine off to enable scanning. The chopping machine, still in use today, resembles a weaving loom, with a mechanical crank to force a guillotine blade through all the pages. This removes the binding and frees the pages so they can pass through a scanner. Today's rapid-feed digital scanners zip through pages as quickly as a top-speed printer. Optical character recognition software then quickly converts the scanned pages into a searchable PDF. The digital file goes to proofreaders in India, who adjust metadata to capture headings and write descriptions of the accompanying images. The loose pages are wrapped in rubber bands and held on a bookshelf, in case a missing page is identified during proofreading. The finished files are made available through the Internet.

Freed from the slow and expensive process of obtaining permissions, Benetech quickly amassed the world's largest collection of books in accessible formats, available through a digital library called Bookshare. The Library of Congress typically produces two thousand audio recordings per year for readers with low vision, especially the elderly. At its highest point, Recording for the Blind and Dyslexic produced seven thousand titles in a year. Benetech's Bookshare service now has close to six hundred thousand titles in its digital library. Each book is available as a digital file in DAISY format. Developed specifically for print-disabled readers, DAISY text can be rendered in large-print, played aloud via text-to-voice, or transferred into braille. Readers with print disabilities can obtain access privileges to the Bookshare digital library in exchange for a fee, often paid by their university or public library.

As publishers gained comfort with Benetech's approach and e-books more generally, many of them came on as partners. HarperCollins signed a partnership agreement in 2005, and a few years later was sending Benetech the e-pub files for thousands of new titles each year. Even though it is not legally required, Benetech continues to follow the permissions route wherever possible. Receiving e-pub files directly from a partnering publisher is dramatically more cost-efficient than having to purchase, chop, and scan printed copies. While establishing partnerships and signing contracts with publishers remains "transactionally expensive," in Fruchterman's words, Benetech gets significant funding from the U.S. Department of Education. When a student needs a book for school and the publisher declines or ignores the permission request, Benetech still falls back on its chop-and-scan technology, protected by the Chafee Amendment. "We have never been sued," Fruchterman says, "but we have been threatened."

International Copyright Solutions

While the Chafee Amendment created immense new opportunities for organizations like Benetech, the law also had its limits. As an act of the U.S. Congress, the Chafee Amendment applied only to activities conducted within the United States. Around 2000, Recording for the Blind and Dyslexic took the decision to end its distribution to Canada, leaving print-disabled readers there without service. "They decided it was a legal risk," Kerscher explains. "I was in the room when the lawyer gave the advice that they should stop distribution." Kerscher was furious that the organization was abandoning readers who depended on it. "I said, just continue what you're doing, nobody will say anything, it will fly under the radar. Nobody was challenging it." Still, he acknowledges, a lawsuit might have gone either way, because Chafee did not securely create a right to distribute internationally.

For many years, Benetech also limited Bookshare's international reach. Fruchterman explains, "the legal constraints of copyright law being a national thing stopped us from serving the world from the inception." Benetech has developed a variety of technological tools to serve social needs, such as software to enable more secure communication between human rights defenders. "Every other project we'd ever done, international users were half of our base within a few years," Fruchterman noted. "Bookshare was the exception, because the Chafee Amendment stops at the water's edge. People called and we could not help them."

Slowly, the organization developed workarounds to be able to serve overseas patrons. One approach was to secure global distribution rights from publishers when signing partnership agreements. Most publishers sign on globally. "The other way was to work on replicating the regime that made Bookshare possible in the United States, to make that an international norm." This effort proved much more difficult than the original passage of the domestic legislation.

Blind groups spent years lobbying for an international treaty at the World Intellectual Property Organization. The goal was to call upon more countries to create legal space for efforts to serve print-disabled readers. The American Federation for the Blind and other groups led the effort. They were amply supported by other NGOs and developing-country governments that saw this as the first step in a larger process of reforming international copyright law to facilitate library and education efforts. The publishing industry was reasonably supportive, but other trade groups bitterly opposed the treaty. They were concerned the effort was a Trojan horse in a larger battle to weaken intellectual property protections. According to Fruchterman: "The number one opposition was the Motion Picture Association of America, followed by the patent holders. They had to be publicly embarrassed into backing off."

The Marrakesh Treaty to Facilitate Access to Published Works for Persons Who Are Blind, Visually Impaired, or Otherwise Print Disabled was adopted in 2013. Five years later, however, advocates were still working to get the United States, Great Britain, and the European Union to ratify the treaty. Fruchterman explains: "The whole key to Marrakesh has been to get a major publishing market to ratify. That is where the money and the books are." The first major breakthrough came in 2017, when the European Union voted to join. Its members were required to comply by 2018. For readers in Africa and Latin America, implementation by France and Spain was particularly important to enabling the use of books in those languages. Also in 2018, the U.S. Senate voted to ratify the Marrakesh treaty. Congress simultaneously updated the Chafee Amendment to include international exchanges. As a result, print-disabled readers in India now enjoy access to Bookshare's full collection, and Spanish-speakers living in the United States can now read accessible books from Spain.

Lessons

Commercial publishers have already proven willing to grant free licenses to nonprofits distributing digital books to disadvantaged populations. Negotiating these publishing partnerships, however, entails significant transaction costs. Getting a publishers' attention, establishing trust, communicating and explaining the request, drafting a contract, having lawyers review it, and following up take significant time and money. It is vastly more efficient for nonprofits to sign a blanket agreement with each publisher than to request permissions on a title-by-title basis. Clearly establishing that such uses are legal even without permission also facilitates such partnerships. This can be done either within the framework of fair use, or by adopting specific copyright exceptions.

As nonprofit publishers and book dealers tackle book hunger, they must keep in mind the special needs of print-disabled readers. A scientific review by the Vision Loss Expert Group estimates that by 2020, 38.5 million people will experience blindness. Visual impairment affects six times as many persons, and hundreds of millions need eyeglasses to read, but cannot get them. Dyslexia International estimates that 700 million people are dyslexic. All together, around one billion children and adults have some kind of print disability. New book files can be intentionally designed to facilitate simple conversion into adaptive formats. Overlooking this design parameter at the start can make it much more difficult to correct the problem later.

It is commonly noted that digital technologies hold particular potential to empower people with disabilities. Far more often than is recognized, inventors with disabilities have themselves been the driving force behind technological developments. George Kerscher developed the first file format capable of rendering a work as text or audio to meet his own needs and those of others facing the same set of challenges. A partnership between Ray Kurzweil and Stevie Wonder produced the first synthesizer that actually sounded like a grand piano. Vint Cerf, one of the "fathers of the Internet," pioneered the early technology underlying email to better communicate with his wife—both had hearing disabilities. Readers with print disabilities were early adopters of books on tape and e-readers decades before most of us knew such things existed. Educational institutions for the blind were the first commercial adopters of flatbed scanners and text-to-speech software. Only later in the long process of development did all these technologies go mainstream, ultimately benefiting hundreds of millions of users.

Significantly, these groundbreaking innovative efforts did not take place in commercial firms, despite the promise of patents for new inventions. The market for solutions specific to readers with disabilities was too small to lure profit-minded entities, even with strong intellectual property protection. Rather, university scientists and nonprofits serving people with disabilities, and individual inventors with disabilities, did the difficult and unprofitable work of pioneering innovation. I call this phenomenon "mission-driven innovation." As the saying goes, "Necessity is the mother of invention." Nonprofits serving readers excluded by mainstream formats and business models are uniquely positioned to do the hard work of developing new technologies and business models. For them, radical innovation in publishing is mission-critical. For organizations whose mission is generating profit, it makes no sense to invest in the costly work of solving such difficult problems. Academics, whose core mission is knowledge, may not always have the drive to see the research through to a practical solution. Successful innovation requires a willingness to push through failure, and the passion and commitment to keep trying decades before financial rewards are possible.

Once the difficult early work is done, mission-driven innovation often goes on to deliver enormous benefits to a much broader user base, and to the profit-minded companies that serve that broad user base. This has proved true with many technologies initially developed to help readers with print disabilities. I predict it will also prove true for the tricks and techniques of book production and distribution that the organizations profiled in this book are pioneering to overcome book hunger.

EIGHT

Fair Use of Existing Books

Can a teacher translate an English-language book into another language in order to share it with his or her students? Can an author or illustrator adapt a famous children's book to make it more multicultural? Can a nonprofit make cheap photocopies of a popular children's book to give away to low-income families? Can libraries loan digital copies of print materials to patrons? The answer depends on the nuances of copyright law in each country.

Copyright exceptions are sometimes quite specific and clearly defined; others are open-ended and subject to broad interpretation. Not every country has exceptions of the second type, but the United States is globally famous for its doctrine of "fair use." Section 107 of U.S. copyright law reads in part:

> the fair use of a copyrighted work, including such use by reproduction in copies . . . for purposes such as criticism, comment, news reporting, teaching (including multiple copies for classroom use), scholarship, or research, is not an infringement of copyright.

One particularly helpful crystallization of the fair use doctrine comes from Judge Pierre Leval, whose writings were foundational in shaping modern fair use law:

> Although no simple definition of fair use can be fashioned, and inevitably disagreement will arise over individual applications, recognition of the function of fair use as integral to copyright's objectives leads to a coherent and useful set of principles. Briefly stated, the use must be of a character that serves the copyright objective of stimulating productive thought and public instruction without excessively diminishing the incentives for creativity.

Or in words the Supreme Court credited to Joseph McDonald: "Take not from others to such an extent and in such a manner that you would be resentful if they so took from you."

Contrary to popular belief, the fact that something is widely done is no assurance that it is legally recognized as fair use. For example, it is common to find videos on

YouTube of people reading children's books aloud. Perhaps the books' publishers view this as fair use. Perhaps they view it as copyright infringement, but tolerate it as good publicity. Behind the scenes, they might have a contractual arrangement with YouTube, getting paid some amount in return for not suing YouTube's users. It is also possible that we are seeing only those instances in which publishers are unaware of the videos, while many more have been removed as a result of publisher complaints. Fair use is not nearly as broad or as clear-cut as most Americans assume, based on simply observing what goes on around them.

A Fair Use Hypothetical

American law professors frequently educate their law students by presenting "hypotheticals." These fictitious fact patterns are designed to help the students explore the application of law to specific circumstances. Law students tend to greatly appreciate this method as providing a clearer picture of how the law actually works than a more abstract explanation. In that spirit, here is an extended hypothetical to illustrate how the fair use doctrine might apply to a potential nonprofit publishing project to address book hunger.

Let us imagine that a major public library in New York ("The Library") wants to create a collection of multilingual picture books for immigrant children to read with their parents. It purchases a single copy of *The Last Stop on Market Street, The Way Home in the Night, I Am Human: A Book of Empathy, The Day You Begin, My Beautiful Birds,* and five other truly outstanding picture books speaking to the diverse experiences of New York's children. A librarian scans each page and uses a software tool to remove the English text from the illustrations. The Library commissions professional translations into a hundred underserved languages, such as Arabic, Bengali, Polish, Igbo, and Khmer. The translated text is then placed back onto the pages with the digital images, and the files are saved. Since ten books were translated into a hundred languages each, one thousand new multilingual titles have been created. The Library's design team is careful to credit the original author, illustrator, and publisher by name, as well as the translators and a few key funders of this effort.

The Library then makes this new multilingual book collection available to its patrons on smartphones and e-readers. Over the next twenty years, these stories are read more than a million times. After tracking digital downloads, the Library also commissions 100,000 hardcover copies of the most popular translations. Of these, 10,000 copies are divided among the local library branches of the New York Public Library and the Brooklyn and Queens library systems. Each site receives only books in those languages that are currently deemed most relevant in its neighborhood, with some extras being stored centrally in anticipation of future requests as neighborhood demographics change. The remaining 90,000 hard copies are delivered to First Book to sell to schools, nonprofits, and libraries in other cities and towns. The resulting income to the Library is enough to fully offset the costs of undertaking the project.

Is this hypothetical project fair use?

Extensive case law establishes that parody and commentary generally qualify as "transformative" fair use. There is no similarly clear line of precedent for nonprofit educational copying. Courts would not have as detailed a road map for how to apply the factors commonly used to evaluate cases where the copier claims fair use. Most judges would concede that the library's "nonprofit educational purpose" is a strong point in its favor. On the other hand, the use of the entire book—rather than a short excerpt—could be construed to weigh heavily against fair use. The ultimate verdict would likely depend on how the court views the potential financial harm to the book's author and publisher. The Library should therefore argue that although a translation into a profitable market such as Spanish could be presumed to be harmful to the copyright holders' economic rights, no such profit opportunity exists in the languages chosen for this project. A very limited potential for market harm, combined with the strong public interest in promoting early literacy, should point to a decision of fair use.

My professional opinion, as someone who teaches copyright law regularly and has studied hundreds of copyright precedents, is that this is the only correct answer for a court to reach, given both the letter and the spirit of copyright law. But other copyright experts might disagree, including perhaps the lawyers representing the authors or publishers of the books chosen for the project. In fair use, there are not guaranteed outcomes, and thus there are no entirely certain predictions. The Library could very reasonably stand on principle to assert fair use, but it would need to be prepared to defend that claim publicly and perhaps even in court. If a publisher or author brought suit, it would likely result in a legal precedent more clearly establishing the mass translation method of addressing book hunger in neglected languages to be fair use. As a bonus, the court might well exercise its discretion to order the losing party to pay the fees of the Library's lawyers. Because of this possibility, as well as the legal and social significance of this case, the Library could probably secure free legal representation.

Since fair use is never certain, though, there would remain a risk, however slight, of an unfavorable decision. In this worst-case scenario, how much financial risk would the Library be exposed to? So long as only ten titles were used, the likely statutory damages range of $750 to $30,000 can be multiplied only ten times. (It is irrelevant whether one hundred or one million copies were made; the statutory damages range is multiplied based on the number of copyrighted titles affected.) This would point to a potential upper limit of $300,000. An award of $7,500 seems much more probable, however, given the sympathetic nature of the Library's activities. Alternatively, the publishers could ask the court to award a fair value for the unauthorized copies. In this case, a court might order the library to pay the same price it normally pays for those titles in English. Since the Library is a nonprofit with a reasonable claim to fair use, the court would probably not award legal fees if the Library ended up on the losing side of the case. Perhaps a charitable foundation would be willing to serve as the Library's insurer for up to the maximum amount of potential damages, to limit the risk to the Library. It would be at the trial judge's discretion whether to enjoin the Library from future efforts along the same lines, or to decline to issue an injunction based on the public interests at stake.

Given that the Library's case for a fair use argument is so strong, children's publishers may well prove willing to grant express permission at no charge. This would allow them to take public credit and earn goodwill for a voluntary contribution to a groundbreaking charitable project. This approach is preferable, from the Library's point of view, because it would completely avoid legal risk. Since the Library only needs ten books and there are many publishers in the country, it could easily wait to see which publishers agree to grant permission before selecting which books to honor in this way. A voluntary partnership would also save the Library the trouble of scanning the book images, since the publishers could provide high-resolution files. The primary benefit of selecting titles without a publisher's collaboration would be if the Library felt it was important to establish the legal precedent that mass translation to alleviate book hunger is fair use. Even without litigation, a voluntary partnership would establish an industry precedent in favor of free licensing. This might ultimately ripen into a clear statutory exception, as with the Chafee Amendment.

Applying this type of analysis internationally is much more complicated. Copyright protection is mandated by international treaties, but exceptions remain optional and vary widely. Not all countries have flexible exceptions like fair use, though interest in adopting them is on the rise. In other countries, mass translation of children's stories into neglected languages could fall under specific exceptions for educational activities. China and Vietnam interpret their educational exceptions very broadly to promote student access to otherwise unaffordable works. India's courts recently deemed university photocopying to be fair in terms more sweeping than would be imaginable in U.S. law. Even Germany, which makes libraries pay for the privilege of loaning out books to blind readers, has recently broadened its educational exceptions, possibly creating room for a project like this. Again, the answer need not be certain to open the door to a friendly negotiation with a publisher for a global charitable license.

Searching for Clarity

The open-endedness of the American fair use exception is both its greatest strength and its greatest weakness. On one hand, having such a general and vague provision allows for flexibility and innovation. Fair use has been successfully invoked to protect parody, political criticism, home VCR recordings, and Internet search engines. The flip side of this flexibility, however, is that the boundaries are unclear. Because the legal test for fair use is so complex, special expertise and careful research are essential to offer a well-grounded opinion on any particular situation. A small change to the hypothetical presented above—such as including Mandarin among the chosen languages for translation—might well lead to a different outcome.

Even experts may reach different opinions on the same set of facts, or have to admit that the outcome is uncertain. David Nimmer, editor of the most authoritative reference work on copyright law, complains that the modern fair use test is "malleable enough to be crafted to fit either point of view." He points out that judges routinely disagree with each other both on individual steps of the test and on the ultimate result. His point is countered by Barton Beebe, a professor at New York University, who has studied hundreds of fair use opinions. Beebe points out that the cases that end up in court naturally tend to be the most difficult ones, which really could go either way. If a use is very likely fair, plaintiffs tend not to sue. If a use is very likely unfair, defendants generally agree to pay rather than press the issue in court.

Other scholars, notably Pamela Samuelson, have identified consistent patterns in fair use decisions. Samuelson notes, however, that copying for educational uses remains particularly unclear. The Supreme Court once accepted a case for appeal in which the National Institutes of Health had photocopied scientific articles for researchers to read.

The Court was unable to reach a majority decision, one justice having recused himself and the others evenly split. Few other cases have ever been decided involving scholarly or educational copying. My own impression of these cases is that U.S. courts tend to find educational copying unfair only if the copier is a commercial entity or otherwise in competition with the original author. Samuelson suggests there are few cases brought against nonprofit educational copying either because publishers accept this as fair use, or because such copying is simply difficult to detect.

My theory is that publishers have long avoided bringing these cases because they dared not take the significant risk of losing. Universities and schools proved willing to pay low licensing fees that collectively have added up to significant income for certain publishers. If courts ever did clearly establish that nonprofit educational photocopying is fair use, this income stream might disappear. Recent developments have forced the issue, however. As universities shifted from paper photocopying to digital course packs, some decided to stop paying the licensing fees. Georgia State University was sued by Cambridge University Press, Oxford University Press, and Sage Publications. Funding to bring the case was provided by the Association of American Publishers and the Copyright

Clearance Center, which clearly understood the importance of the precedent the case would set. After several years and several hundred pages of trial and appeals court opinions in *Cambridge University Press v. Patton*, the university's course packets were held to be mostly fair. The university was awarded more than $3 million in legal fees, at the publishers' expense. The court ordered the university only to further encourage faculty compliance with fair use guidelines.

Risk Mitigation

Organizations focused on global book hunger should give greater attention to the possibility of adapting existing titles to their purposes. Translation into neglected languages for educational purposes is likely fair use, with no permission or payment required. To stay on the right side of the law, nonprofits should be sure to demonstrate good faith by retaining the book's copyright notice, the names of the author and illustrator, and the original publisher. Recoloring a well-known picture book's images to "diversify" its white characters would likely also be deemed fair use. So would altering the text of an outdated children's book to retell the story from another perspective. All of these strategies remain to be tried. For most nonprofits in the literacy space, however, copyright litigation is neither on brand nor on mission. It may take a library, a law school, or a specially created nonprofit to push the legal envelope.

Another route is for book nonprofits to work on establishing voluntary fair use guidelines specific to their field. Scholars Patricia Aufderheide and Peter Jazsi first innovated this approach by helping to produce the Documentary Filmmakers' Statement About Best Practices in Fair Use. This document was developed by documentary filmmakers and copyright lawyers, without the participation of third parties. Once the best practices guidelines were released, insurance companies became much more willing to offer litigation insurance to documentary filmmakers. Aufderheide and Jazsi's book, *Reclaiming Fair Use: How to Put Balance Back in Copyright,* also details how seven other creative communities worked to develop similar codes of conduct. These voluntary codes help to establish consensus over appropriate boundaries for fair use in each particular context. An even more recent example, the Position Statement on Controlled Digital Lending, seeks to define restrictions for libraries lending digital materials online.

As publishers ultimately weigh whether to give or withhold permission in response to translation requests, or possibly even file suit, I would urge them to take a historical perspective. In the 1980s, the U.S. film industry fought to block home video recording equipment, which it viewed as a threat to its copyrights. After the Supreme Court deemed these technologies protected by fair use, however, home video became extremely profitable for the film industry. Similarly, without the innovative efforts of George Kerscher and others to develop digital audio formats for blind readers, commercial publishers might never have discovered the profit potential of audio books. Billions of potential future consumers currently cannot buy books. Empowering nonprofits to experiment and find solutions for hard-to-reach readers is very much in the long-term interest of commercial publishing.

NINE

New Copyright Exceptions

The nonprofit organization Benetech operates many programs turning technology to social benefit. The biggest part of this work is Bookshare, an adaptive-format digital library for people with blindness and other print disabilities. CEO Jim Fruchterman spent more than a year fighting for international adoption of the Marrakesh Treaty to facilitate cross-border sharing between such libraries. He is keenly aware of how copyright law can limit the possibilities for addressing book hunger through innovative nonprofit efforts. "Many things are possible, but not permitted to exist," Fruchterman explains. "We could push a different button and make Bookshare the free library for poor people in any country." As the law currently stands, however, doing so would create too much legal risk for Benetech.

Some U.S. publishers would see such a move as fair use. Others would view it as copyright infringement. Since any publisher whose books appear in the library would have standing to sue, chances are good that one or more would. Even assuming a judge would ultimately find in the charity's favor, there might still be negative consequences. The mere accusation of illegal activity could hurt the charity's fundraising and relationships with publishers. The organization would have to hire lawyers, and reimbursement of legal fees is not guaranteed, even if they ultimately won in court. Litigation would also be a time-consuming distraction from the central mission. Since fair use is an inherently uncertain defense, there is also the risk of losing the case.

For Benetech, this risk is dramatically increased by the way that damages would be calculated. Under U.S. copyright law, a publisher may insist on statutory damages ranging from $750 to $30,000, even without proving financial harm. A large charity like Benetech might decide it could afford to take this risk if the worst-case scenario was a $30,000 fine. Unfortunately, that is not the relevant limit. Courts have repeatedly interpreted the statute to multiply this range by the number of copyrighted works.

Since the Bookshare library contains more than 600,000 books, the low end of this range would be $750 multiplied by 600,000. That means the *lowest* possible award would be $450 million. A jury could take the award as high as $30,000 times 600,000, or $18 *billion*. The absurdity of this result highlights the need to reform U.S. statutory damages rules. This type of multiplication was never intended by lawmakers, and flies in the face of longstanding doctrines of legal fairness, but it may take an act of Congress or a Supreme Court decision to reverse such a well-settled practice.

Even with bankruptcy on the line, however, Benetech can be confident in its ability to legally serve printdisabled readers. The Chafee Amendment of 1996 clearly establishes that "it is not an infringement of copyright" for a nonprofit organization serving disabled readers to copy and distribute books "in specialized formats exclusively for use by blind or other persons with disabilities." This provides Benetech and other organizations like it with much greater certainty than relying on fair use. Publishers similarly know exactly where they stand, allowing them to avoid the expense of researching every author's contract to see if they are permitted to share files with Benetech. The possibility of expensive litigation is avoided on all sides.

The Chafee Amendment is a highly successful example of a specific copyright exception passed to help address book hunger. Without it, Benetech might never have come into existence. Because of this legal safe harbor, a new model of delivering books to a book hungry population was made possible. We should build on this past success by enacting additional copyright exceptions to address book hunger beyond the blind and print-disabled population.

What Are Copyright Exceptions?

Publishers themselves wrote the first copyright exception into international copyright treaties. Realizing how impractical it could be to seek permission from fellow publishers when quoting brief excerpts of their work, they included a requirement in the Berne Convention for the Protection of Literary Works in 1886 that all countries enact a "quotation" exception. To date, quotation and disability accommodation are the only exceptions required by international law, but many more are permitted.

Specific copyright exceptions are sometimes enacted in response to public pressure. In 1996, journalist Elisabeth Bumiller reported that the American Society of Composers and Publishers had sent letters to thousands of summer camps, asking them to pay licensing fees of $250 and up for performance rights to its songs. Exaggerated reports soon followed that ASCAP was threatening to sue the Girl Scouts for singing around the campfire. Congress amended the law to prevent any such result. The Girl Scouts can now sing for free, thanks to a specific copyright exception for musical performances by "scouting and fraternal groups," 17 U.S. Code section 110(10).

Specific exceptions are a common and time-honored method of tailoring copyright law to preserve incentives for creativity while permitting harmless or socially beneficial uses. For example, section 109 of the U.S. copyright statute permits the resale of used books, and section 110(3) permits unlicensed performances in religious services. French copyright law has an exception specifically permitting artistic expression through *pastiche*, an artistic work that mimics the style of another artist, period, or work of art; whereas parody uses imitation to poke fun or mock, pastiche celebrates the art or artist that it imitates. Brazil has an exception authorizing photographs and paintings of statues located in public places. Germany guarantees "freedom of panorama" with a specific exception authorizing photography of architectural works. Copyright exceptions to assist schools, universities, libraries, museums, and other cultural institutions are also common in many countries.

Copyright exceptions can be structured either as a "free pass" or as a paid license. American law tends to follow the first approach. Most uses falling within our exceptions—including resale of second-hand books, library lending, conversion to accessible formats, archiving, and brief quotation—do not require any payment. Music is an important exception to this general rule. Here, the U.S. Copyright Act empowers an administrative body to set standard compensation rates. Musicians may record any song, so long as they pay a predetermined rate. DJs similarly obtain permission to play music at weddings and other live events through the compulsory licensing exception. (Music streaming, as well as soundtracks for film and television, fall outside of this framework and must be specially negotiated.)

Some other countries make greater use of paid approaches. Germany's copyright act has long obliged libraries, even those serving blind readers, to pay 11.50 euros per book on their shelves, in addition to the price of purchase. Another rule common in Europe requires painters to be paid a fair share when their artwork is resold. Paid exceptions like these can enhance creators' income while avoiding the need for costly negotiations. In charitable settings, however, paying royalties inevitably takes funds away from the organization's social mission. Recognizing this, U.S. copyright law specifically exempts nonprofit musical and theater performances from the need to license the plays they perform, without any payment obligation. Paid exceptions also come with administrative costs. Special bodies must be staffed, economic studies commissioned, and negotiations conducted among interest groups. In weaker democracies, collection agencies have been prone to corruption, diverting the funds intended to benefit creators. With any paid exception, moreover, the user must apply for permission, pay fees, and keep records. In the United States, a nonprofit unaware of the requirement to pay would face litigation and the threat of statutory damages.

Whether free or paid, copyright exceptions are central to accommodating public interests in copyright law. Harvard copyright scholar Ruth Okediji identifies them as the most important legal tool to promote access to knowledge. At the World Intellectual Property Organization (WIPO), the global body for negotiation of new copyright treaties, representatives of developing countries also view exceptions as critical. The Marrakesh Treaty was the first to require countries to create copyright exceptions. With its passage, WIPO has taken up debate on a new treaty regarding library exceptions. Next, the organization is likely to focus on exceptions to promote education.

Exceptions to address book hunger could be incorporated into either of these treaties.

Safeguards for Authors and Publishers

Over the past decade, WIPO's efforts to expand copyright exceptions, as well as protections, have proven controversial. Industry groups that depend on copyright protection fear a slippery slope. Will narrow exceptions for compelling public interests, such as access to books for the print-disabled, gradually lead to broader exceptions that erode profits? One powerful safeguard against such an outcome is the World Trade Organization (WTO) Agreement on Trade-Related Aspects of Intellectual Property (TRIPs). TRIPs limits copyright exceptions to "certain special cases which do not conflict with a normal exploitation of the work and do not unreasonably prejudice the legitimate interests of the right holder." In other words, exceptions must be carefully tailored to achieve their public interest goals without harming authors and publishers.

There are several ways to achieve this tailoring when looking at the problem of book hunger. The most secure way to protect authors and publishers, while addressing book hunger, is by treating different languages differently. The current copyright regime has worked extraordinarily well to produce works in English, French,

German, Spanish, and so on. No legal changes are needed in those language markets. Copyright exceptions should be targeted to facilitate and encourage translations into neglected languages. By definition, expanding charitable efforts in neglected languages does not endanger publishing profits. These languages are neglected precisely because they are unprofitable.

Pharmaceutical companies have strongly resisted patent exceptions that would lower prices on drugs in developing countries. They understandably worry that discounted medicines in poorer countries would find their way back to consumers in wealthier countries. They probably also fear public pressure for price-regulating legislation, if American patients realize they are paying thousands of dollars for the same medication that Thai patients can purchase for next to nothing. Government price controls are already the reality in Europe and Canada.

Similar concerns can also apply to books. In *Kirtsaeng v. John Wiley, Inc.*, the U.S. Supreme Court rejected a publisher's effort to bar its own cheaply printed mathematics textbooks sold in Thailand from being resold to American students. Importantly, both versions of these textbooks were in English; American students would have no interest in textbooks printed in the Central Thai language. Similarly, donating Ndebele-language children's books to schools in South Africa will not undermine those titles' English-language sales. Language offers a way of perfectly segmenting the market for books, allowing one price to prevail here and another there. If only we had such a simple solution for patented medications!

Why Translation Exceptions?

Children's picture books play a key role in developing early literacy, yet most of the more than 560 languages used in primary education have a grossly inadequate supply. As I argue in the final chapter, the only hope of meeting this need is through a mass translation effort. The work of creating an illustrated children's book is overwhelmingly in the story's conception, illustration, and book design. A commercial publisher might spend $10,000 to $20,000 to develop a new premium children's book. Translators Without Borders can facilitate a charitable translation for around $50.

The efficiency of the translation approach is greatly reduced, however, if charities have to clear copyright for each title they translate. Requesting, negotiating, paying for, and keeping track of copyright permissions takes significant time, and therefore money, even when the publisher receives no payment. Commercial publishers working in profitable language markets can afford these significant transaction costs. Charities working in neglected languages cannot. A specific copyright exception to permit charitable translation of children's literature would eliminate this problem. Such an exception would also spare commercial publishers the burden of researching thousands of contracts to verify whether they even have these rights to give away.

A second compelling context for translation exceptions has to do with the rise of increasingly sophisticated automatic translation software. Machine-learning techniques developed by Google in 2016 already translate between English, French, and Spanish with near-human accuracy. As the technology improves, functionality is being added for additional languages. Someday, entire libraries of informational and educational materials will be instantly translatable into a broad array of languages. But will it be legal to do so? A copyright exception for machine translation can eliminate legal risk that may otherwise hamper faster development and deployment of this technology.

A third approach to translation exceptions could help promote newly flourishing literatures in disadvantaged languages. This broader option would not be limited to children's books, but simply establish that "it is not an infringement of copyright to reproduce, distribute, adapt, perform, or stream a work in a neglected language, so long as the contributions of the original creators are credited in good faith." Each country would then specify which of their languages qualify for this special treatment. For example, South Africa might apply the exception to Ndebele, Tsonga, Venda, Xhosa, Zulu, and other indigenous languages. Copyright rules would remain unchanged for works published in English, or other languages with functioning publishing industries. A project that involved translating a Zulu text into English would require permission, expanding opportunities for minority-language authors and publishers to earn income through English translations. In neglected languages, however, textbooks, storybooks, poetry, news, and novels could be freely translated and copied.

A Bit of History

The problem a translation exception is designed to solve did not always exist. In the mid-nineteenth century, copyright law both in the United States and abroad regarded translations as independent new works. All rights in the translated work were held by the translator, who did not require permission from the original author or publisher. Over the next fifty years, European publishers pushed for international treaty provisions to forbid translation without a license. The proposal made sense in the European context. An Italian publisher, for instance, could realize significant income by licensing translations into English, French, and German. Elsewhere in the world, however, the proposal made much less sense.

According to scholar Lionel Bentley, Indian authorities strenuously opposed limits on freedom of translation. They understood that translation of educational and scientific works into local languages was essential to economic progress. Such translations were not commercially viable, but were commonly facilitated by missionary and government efforts. India was still a colony of Britain at the time, however, and its representatives had very little influence on the treaty negotiations. The provisions negotiated among the European countries were made binding on India as well. The Indian Copyright Act of 1914 instituted a new requirement of permission and payment for all translations. This also applied retroactively to already published works.

India's development might have been greatly accelerated had copyright lawyers of that time considered treating different languages differently. Indian authors writing in local languages were rightly concerned with rights to authorize and profit from English translations of their works. Bently notes that this included Rabindranath Tagore, recently awarded the Nobel Prize for his poetry, sensitively translated from Bengali into English. Publishers also hoped that the Indian-language markets would someday become a source of profit for them, although that prospect has not been realized in the intervening century. To this day, educational opportunity in India remains sharply limited by the student's mastery of English.

A half century after the international translation right was adopted, newly independent nations in Africa and Asia also called for modifications to copyright law for developing economies. European, North American, and Australian publishers disapproved. Contentious negotiations through the 1960s produced the international Stockholm Protocol. On its face, the protocol appeared to facilitate translations for developing countries. In practice, it created a permissions process so complicated it was impossible to utilize. Not a single book was ever translated under its authority.

Fast-forward an additional fifty years, and the issue of translation rights came up again as the Marrakesh Treaty for Visually Impaired Persons was being negotiated. The final treaty, however, simply avoided dealing with this issue. It can arguably be interpreted to authorize translations for print-disabled readers, but this is far from clear. As written, the Marrakesh Treaty seems destined to primarily benefit print-disabled readers who speak English,

French, Spanish, or Portuguese—those languages with significant cross-border publishing industries. Yet blindness is much more common in developing countries, where readers require charitable translations.

Recommendations

Copyright law is fundamental to the livelihood of commercial publishers. Even with strong copyright protection and anti-piracy efforts, however, there are contexts in which publishers will never be able to make a profit. This is particularly true with niche markets, such as specialized formats for disabled readers and languages spoken predominantly by the poor. In the next decade, I would like to see copyright law become more carefully tailored to preserve financial incentives for profitable publishing, while encouraging charitable and government efforts to adapt existing works for underserved readers. Mass translation of children's literature into neglected languages is a powerful strategy to end book hunger, if it is clearly permitted. Some countries could go even further, specifying lists of neglected languages, in which works of any genre may freely be translated and reproduced. Machine translation technology should also be encouraged, including by providing a safe harbor from copyright liability.

In recent years, the Marrakesh Treaty provided important support for the global spread of copyright exceptions for the blind. Translation exceptions would also benefit from a coordinated international effort. WIPO's anticipated treaty negotiations on copyright exceptions for library and educational uses present golden opportunities to address book hunger. To avoid the international disagreements that have historically plagued copyright treaties, new exceptions for translation must explicitly recognize that different languages have different market realities. Where a flourishing publishing industry exists, current rules should remain unchanged. In the American saying: "If it ain't broke, don't fix it." Neglected languages are deserving of special treatment, however, to boost opportunities for their speakers.

TEN

Choosing Open Licenses

In its first ten years, the nonprofit Pratham Books produced around 450 children's titles. In the next two years, it created 7,000. The key to this explosion of creativity was the charity's new online platform, StoryWeaver. Here, dozens of colorful thumbnail images each point to a delightfully illustrated children's story. A filter allows visitors to quickly find all the works in a particular language, such as English (2,984 titles), Hindi (1,101), French (682), or Bengali (248). Each story may be read online, shared on Facebook or Twitter, saved for offline reading, and downloaded for printing. The key innovation of StoryWeaver, however, is that visitors can also adapt existing stories to create new ones. Thanks to a user-friendly interface, anyone who can browse the web and edit slides can create a beautifully illustrated children's story, with no artistic talent required. Native English speakers can easily "relevel" an advanced story for younger readers by simplifying the text. Bilingual visitors can translate stories into a new language. The truly ambitious can create an entirely new story, drawing on a bank of more than ten thousand child-friendly illustrations.

This adaptability is the secret to the recent explosion in productivity. Originally, Pratham Books relied on the efforts of its hired authors, illustrators, and translators. StoryWeaver is premised on the observation that large numbers of people each dedicating a little free time can often do a job more efficiently than full-time staff. Wikipedia became the world's largest encyclopedia and YouTube became the second-most visited website in the world by enabling what Yochai Benkler's *The Wealth of Networks* identifies as "peer production." Peer production began among software engineers, but has grown into a significant model of creative production in the era of social media. These collaborative platforms provide an outlet for individual creativity, technological tools to make the production process simple, and the psychic motivation of being able to reach a vast audience.

Creative Commons

StoryWeaver's openness to follow-on creativity is made possible by Creative Commons licenses. Copyright law establishes that every recorded work of art, music, or writing is automatically protected for the lifetime of the creator plus an additional fifty years. During this time, no one may copy, translate, or build upon that work without the explicit permission of the copyright holder, unless a statutory exception applies. Creators who actually *want* to see their work shared, translated, or built upon, however, can give back some of these exclusive rights by attaching a Creative Commons license. This lets others know that they have the author's advance permission to do certain types of things with the work. Ownership of the copyright stays in the name of the author; the Creative Commons license operates like a rider or addendum.

Creative Commons licenses are an outgrowth of the open-source software movement. Historically, most software was free for copying, sharing, and building upon. This changed in the 1970s and 1980s as software became included under copyright law. Some computer programmers disliked the shift. The new proprietary approach made it harder for them to get their hands on code that they could use, explore, and adapt to new purposes. Richard Stallman and Linus Torvalds were leaders in the effort to recover the original approach. Gradually, open-source software advocates agreed on standard licensing terms to ensure the openness and interoperability of the code they produced. Today, open-source and proprietary software both play important roles in the computer industry.

In the late 1990s and early 2000s, others began to adapt the idea of open licensing beyond software. The Open Content License was created in 1998 to enable sharing of text, music, and art. Wikipedia launched in 2001, built around a GNU Free Documentation License, to ensure that its articles could be freely edited. In 2005, the Hewlett Foundation gave Larry Lessig and collaborators at Stanford Law School a grant of $1 million to develop an even more robust set of open content licenses. These Creative Commons licenses are now the leading standard in open licensing.

What began as a small movement of people who believed in sharing has grown into a significant force. Open licensing has become standard in many academic disciplines, from physics to medicine. Services such as Flickr and Google now allow users to search specifically for openly licensed photographs and video. By 2016, authors, musicians, and other creative types had used Creative Commons licenses to share more than 1.2 *billion* creations.

Open licensing is particularly ideal for creators more interested in exposure than earnings.

Open Translation

About ten years ago, SooHyun Pae was preparing for a career as a translator between Korean (her native language) and English. Then she discovered the Creative Commons movement. "It helped me a lot, understanding translation as a creative work itself." Under copyright law, a translation into another language is considered a "derivative work," which can only be done with the explicit permission of the original author. "Translation is a derivative work of another creative work," Pae acknowledges, "but I felt, and I still feel, that translation is itself the creative work of a translator."

As a full-time creator of new works out of old ones, Pae easily recognized the power of Creative Commons licenses. "If you allow more derivative works to be created, it helps to enrich the culture in many different languages." Creative Commons licenses acknowledge the work of the original author; they also "appreciate peoples' efforts and interest in making use of creative works to create another creative work," in Pae's words. Pae also saw open translation as offering an important opportunity to promote cross-cultural understanding. "When you translate something, it's not just using different language to deliver the same message to a different audience. It's about connecting two different cultures and interacting with people from other cultures, trying to understand other cultures."

Today, Pae is a leader in South Korea's Creative Commons community. Her current projects include advising a nonprofit that translates foreign children's books to increase Korean children's exposure to other cultures, as well as translating texts about open licensing and free culture into Korean. Pae articulates the broader philosophical foundations behind the free culture movement. "When I first joined this movement, I was into this concept of giving access to information and creativity to everyone." This can indeed be an important function of Creative Commons licensing. "But nowadays," Pae continues, "I feel it's more about giving everyone the opportunity to engage and participate." Not just as a reader or consumer, Pae emphasizes, but truly enabling everyone to take on a creative role. That more active vision of creativity is also a more inclusive one. "We can use Creative Commons licenses to create more materials in diverse languages," Pae says; "I think this could be a huge help."

Organizations focused on overcoming language barriers to reading have enthusiastically embraced open licensing.

Both Pratham Books and the African Storybook Project publish everything they create on Creative Commons licenses. This decision enables educators across the globe to translate any of their materials into any other language. Suzanne Singh of Pratham Books offers an example: "There is a group in the extreme north of India that speak a language called Ladakhi, a hill language." Volunteers in the community converted a number of Pratham Books titles into Ladakhi to use in their schools. This unanticipated use helped to advance the mission of Pratham Books, but would have been impossible for the organization to accomplish directly. "There are 20,000 people speaking the Ladakhi language," Singh points out. "That is not a viable market even for Pratham Books." While producing books in Ladakhi was not high on the agenda for Pratham Books, it was important to people in that community. All they needed was permission.

Additional Advantages

Open-access publishing also helps social publishers address the challenge of affordability. The term "free culture" plays on a double meaning: free as in freedom (*libre*), and free as in "free of charge" (*gratis*). Books with Creative Commons licenses are free in both senses. Parents, teachers, and students may download them to any device without paying a fee. The license also permits local print-ing or photocopying, enabling an at-cost print version.

Recognizing the potential cost savings, the Hewlett Foundation has funded Creative Commons to work on a project to improve the affordability of higher education. In a recent survey, only one-third of U.S. faculty mem-bers reported that at least 90 percent of their students purchased the required textbook. Textbook cost can be a significant barrier to learning. In the United States, esti-mates of college textbook costs range from $655 to $1,300 per year. This might be one-fourth of the total cost of studying at a community college. Creative Commons now promotes the goal of a Zero Textbook Cost Degree. Both California and New York have budgeted funds to support the development of openly licensed textbooks. Faculty authors are compensated for their work through an up-front grant. Students nationally are already saving millions of dollars per year by using open textbooks.

Creative Commons licenses also facilitate adaptation into other formats. Openly licensed textbooks enable fac-ulty members to adjust or recombine existing materials for different courses. Openly licensed stories can be re-corded in audio or audiovisual formats, reformatted for blind or dyslexic students, or releveled to make advanced texts simpler for early learners. Without an open license, educators wanting to do any of these things for their students face daunting questions. Is it fair use or not? Is it worth writing and waiting for permission? What if payment is requested that makes it no longer worthwhile? In some cases, copyright savvy or pure persistence wins out, but many other opportunities are lost.

Choosing Among License Options

I tell my students to think of open licenses like ice cream: they come in a variety of flavors. Then I share a personal story to illustrate the point. I first began using Creative Commons licenses in 2006. I had gone for a walk across the University of Chicago campus on a beautiful September day. I happened to walk past Frank Lloyd Wright's Robie House. Having recently bought a digital camera for graduation, I snapped several pictures of the historic building. Later, I uploaded the photos to Flickr, selecting the option to attach a Creative Commons license. Months later, I received a thank-you email; one of my photos had been used in a university publication by my alma mater. My photography skills are very amateur, but my work met their need, saving someone a long walk on a cold day.

Creative Commons licenses come with options. The creator can choose to require attribution or not, to forbid changes or not, and to bar or permit commercial use. For my early Flickr experiment, I chose the Attribution Share-Alike license, abbreviated as CC-BY-SA. The terms of this license required the University of Chicago to credit me as the photographer, and to share its own resulting publication on a similar license. I had decided against the "no derivatives" restriction, because I had no objection to my photos being cropped or converted to black-and-white. I also avoided the "no commercial use" restriction, because I would have been fine with seeing the photo appear in a commercial tourism brochure or coffee table book.

Today, Creative Commons encourages its users to choose its simplest licenses, because every restriction limits the work's potential usefulness. For example, a "no derivatives" restriction would prohibit translations or excerpts. Google Books will not carry the full text of books published with a "no commercial use" restriction. A "share alike" provision could deter a commercial publisher from making copies available in print. Creative Commons has two licenses, however, that are compatible with all of these uses. Under the elegantly simple CC-BY license, attribution to the original creator is the only requirement. When even credit is unimportant, the creator can go further, selecting a CC0 license to dedicate the work to the public domain. Those options may not be best in every circumstance. This book, for instance, carries a Creative Commons-Attribution-Noncommercial-ShareAlike (CC-BY-NC-SA) license. This authorizes personal copying and charitable translation, while protecting Yale University Press from competition.

Getting Started

Creative Commons licensing has a vital role to play in tackling book hunger. Open-access books facilitate cost-less sharing and adaptation to diverse needs, especially through translation. Although open licensing is not right for everyone, I believe that all authors, illustrators, and publishers with a sense of social mission should explore what open licensing could do for their cause.

Open licensing mandates are also becoming increasingly common requirements for funding from governments and foundations. Mandates certainly have power to quickly transform a field, but I would prefer to see this happen through encouragement rather than by force. Funders can incentivize authors and publishers to learn about and experiment with open licensing. Book charities themselves are smart to get ahead of the curve. This is possible even when the charity or author does not have complete control over the copyright. When I have asked my publishers to agree to Creative Commons licenses on my articles and books, better than nine out of ten have agreed.

Charities experienced with Creative Commons licensing recommend starting out small. Intellectual property lawyer Gautam John first suggested that Pratham Books experiment with Creative Commons licenses in 2008. Pratham Books implemented the suggestion by putting just a few titles on open licenses. "The response to this was phenomenal," Suzanne Singh recounts. "People picked up our books and translated them into new languages. The content got repurposed; teachers were using it in different ways." There was also an impact on print sales. "We were concerned it would cannibalize the sales," John notes, "but the books we had made available online outsold the books we had not three-to-one." "It's not really counterintuitive," John argues, noting that many other content creators have witnessed similar results. "This is free advertising of a kind."

Open licensing requires a counterintuitive leap of faith: that surrendering control will actually help achieve your goals. The best way to overcome doubt is to conduct your own experiment. If you are a publisher, identify half a dozen backlist titles whose sales have slowed, and release half of them on a Creative Commons license. If you are an author, identify two books with similar sales figures and ask your publisher to put just one on an open license. You may find, as Pratham Books did, that print sales increase for the open book, because digital circulation is serving as free marketing. Although it is more difficult to track, there should also be a positive impact on sales of non-open titles by the same author. If you are a creator, you are likely to receive more invitations to illustrate, or speak publicly, as more people discover your work. Open up your creativity to others, and see what happens.

ELEVEN

Rethinking Incentives

"No man but a blockhead ever wrote, except for money." Though frequently misattributed to Mark Twain, this is actually a quotation from Samuel Johnson, the author of the first dictionary of the English language. The experience of Iceland, however, casts Johnson's claim into serious doubt. With only 350,000 speakers, the potential readership for Icelandic books is truly minuscule; yet Iceland's publishing scene is thriving. One in ten Icelanders will publish in their lifetime, according to an article in *BBC Magazine* by Rosie Goldsmith. An Icelandic phrase translates literally as "Everyone has a book in their stomach." Are Icelandic writers and publishers somehow managing to turn a profit against long odds? Or do they write, edit, and publish for other reasons?

I asked experts on Iceland's publishing scene for their views on Samuel Johnson's blockhead quote. Egill Johannsson, chairman of the Icelandic Publishers Association, paused, puzzled by the question. "I don't think that applies to Icelandic authors," Johannsson finally replied. "I don't relate to those words at all. From my knowing a lot of authors, both Icelandic and foreign, I have yet to meet the author that writes for money." Baldur Bjarnason, a graduate of the University of Iceland's literature program and publishing industry consultant, was even more blunt. Bjarnason let loose a long and hearty laugh, before composing himself for a proper response: "No. Icelandic writers don't set out to make a living. Nobody writes for money."

Both men report that only a handful of authors in Iceland earn a living from royalties. These are mostly crime novelists who signed good contracts for translations into German and French. Perhaps another dozen authors benefit from a government stipend that funds a year of full-time writing. These are the exceptions, however, rather than the rule. "Writing needs a day job," Bjarnason states emphatically. Despite the low financial prospects, Iceland's publishing scene is thriving. "Icelandic authors have a passion for writing," Johannsson says. "They have a passion to be heard. That's why they write." Bjarnason agrees and identifies a second reason: the financial incentives may not be high, but the barriers are extremely low. In Iceland, he says, "It's extremely easy for anybody to find somebody who's capable of doing an editorial read of a text or to give you feedback on narrative structure." It is also easy to find a publisher, or to self-publish. "There are two ways to express yourself in Iceland," Bjarnason claims. "One is writing a book and the other is forming a band. The one thing those two share is that there's an easily accessible infrastructure and expertise."

Iceland's publishers may be more profit-minded than its authors. "They are trying to make money," Bjarnason believes. "They try and they fail." Johannsson, head of Iceland's largest publishing house, Forlagid, disagrees. Although the company does make a profit, Johannsson denies this is the goal. "We don't do it for profit. We use the money we profit to invest in more publishing, doing what we love to do. That is very publisher-like to use the money you make to publish something else you love." Few other Icelandic publishers turn a profit. Johannsson generalizes: "Is publishing in Icelandic profitable? No. Nobody enters publishing to get rich. . . . But you have the benefit of doing something that is extremely nice and fun to do. And if you have a passion for it, it's the best thing to do in the world."

(Dis)incentivizing Authorship

It might seem obvious that financial incentives will motivate more of the incentivized behavior. A moment's reflection, however, reveals that the relationship between incentives and behavior is more complicated. In many cases, people are motivated to do things without any financial incentives. For example, most people fall in love and raise children without being paid to do so. This is referred to as *intrinsic motivation;* the incentive comes from the activity itself. When Johannsson says that Icelanders write and publish because "they have a passion for it," because it is "what we love to do," "extremely nice and fun," even "the best thing to do in the world," he is identifying intrinsic motivations.

For her book *The Eureka Myth,* legal scholar Jessica Silbey extensively interviewed artists and scientists about the motivations for their work. Novelists and painters, journalists and computer scientists—all reported that internal motivations are more powerful than money. Silbey found that successful creators are initially inspired by serendipity and a sense of play, focus more on the process than the outcome, and are motivated by notions of rhythm, artistic integrity, and community-building. She concludes that intrinsic motivations, rather than financial ones, power most creativity. "The emotional and personal rewards derived from these commitments eclipse the financial payoffs of the work, be they uncertain or robust," Silbey writes.

While pleasure is obviously a primary motivation for reading, we might not expect the same to be true for writing, because it is more difficult. Writing a book may be a source of greater psychological satisfaction than simply reading one, however, precisely because it is more difficult. Psychologist Reed Larson studied how the emotional state of "flow" affects the writing process. Bored writers, he found, were unable to find challenge and excitement in their projects and produced dull writing that was unenjoyable to read. It is not simply a question of being interested in one's topic; the writer must also work to find an appropriate level of challenge in the task, neither too high nor too low. In this state, Larson explains, an author can enjoy the excitement of guiding the project to a successful conclusion.

Psychologist Edward Deci suggests that human beings are intrinsically motivated to select and complete challenging creative tasks because of our deep need to feel autonomous and competent. He hypothesized that external rewards could have the unintended consequence of undermining these motivations. A great number of studies he and others later conducted found precisely this impact. "Careful consideration of reward effects reported in 128 experiments leads to the conclusion that tangible rewards tend to have a substantially negative effect on intrinsic motivation" for people who were originally highly motivated to perform a task they saw as enjoyable, Deci and his coauthors concluded in *A Meta-Analytic Review of Experiments Examining the Effect of Extrinsic Rewards on Intrinsic Motivation.* This "disincentive effect" is strongest when the external reward is financial. In contrast, praise can reinforce intrinsic motivation.

The counterproductive effect of financial rewards is strongest for activities that people find psychologically rewarding because they are fun, culturally valued, or otherwise meaningful. Writing can be enjoyable on all these dimensions. An author can experience the writing process as play, in which the creator enjoys a high degree of control over the outcome. Having a book published tends to make people feel proud of their accomplishment. An author may also feel gratified for having made a contribution to society, advancing knowledge in an area that one cares about, or the pure satisfaction of self-expression. Moreover, society praises certain activities precisely because they are socially valuable, yet not very lucrative. To the extent that people internalize the notion that doing something for profit makes it less praiseworthy, being financially rewarded may undermine the sense of pride or virtue associated with it.

Millions of Blockheads

If research on creative motivation is correct, Icelandic authors are in fact highly fortunate. From the beginning, they start with no expectation of a financial reward. They know they are writing for expression, enjoyment, and esteem. The resulting book is a source of satisfaction and pride even if it sells only fifteen copies. The financial prospects for English-language writers are substantially more promising. Because the American novelist expects to make money, however, a modest royalty check may be perceived as a discouraging negative indicator of competence, undermining intrinsic motivation. The elusive prospect of fame and money can be a double-edged sword. Past financial success can also heighten the sense of pressure to deliver an even more successful next book. The opposite of flow is "writer's block," when an author is so anxious over whether the current project will be successful that he or she experiences a creative shutdown. "I feel this way all the time," admitted best-selling author John Green, who placed second on the list of highest-paid authors when *The Fault in Our Stars* came out on film. Green beat long odds; even in America, most books sell fewer than five hundred copies. Green's advice on handling writer's block, as quoted by Julie Bort in *Business Insider,* echoes the psychological literature on intrinsic motivation. "The only way through it for me is to take pleasure in the process of writing. The act of writing for an audience must feel valuable in and of itself, or else I am doomed." In between episodes of financial success, or in its absence, authors must draw upon deeper motivations—such as pleasure, self-expression, writer's high, public appreciation, a sense of calling or of giving a gift to the world—to fuel their art.

According to U.S. census data, only a few hundred Americans identify themselves as independent authors. Across all stages of their careers, they report an average income of $60,000, just 20 percent more than the typical *starting* salary of a recent college graduate. Writers looking for monetary rewards do not write books; they write catalog copy, corporate policy manuals, press releases, and legal documents. "There's a reason most well-known writers still teach English," novelist Patrick Wensink warns. "Even when there's money in writing, there's not much money." J. K. Rowling bought a castle thanks to her top-selling Harry Potter books, but she is literally one in a million. Choosing to become a full-time author is like any other career in the arts. A few stars do extremely well financially; many more are "starving artists."

Meanwhile, approximately 1.7 million faculty members at U.S. colleges and universities write books and journal articles in addition to their teaching responsibilities. It is extremely rare for an academic to earn significant income from royalties. We write to solve challenging problems, to influence others with our ideas, and to enhance our professional reputations. Even more people publish their writing for free. On the Tumblr platform alone, there were approximately 400 million blogs as of 2018. Wordpress, another online platform for publishing unpaid content, boasts more than 87 million new posts each month.

Money cannot be the primary reason that millions of people write books and hundreds of millions create blogs. Something other than royalties is motivating the overwhelming majority of authors, even in the world's most lucrative languages. Authors write to express themselves, to communicate ideas, to experience a challenge, and because writing is fun. We might land closer to the truth by editing Johnson's famous words to read: "Only a blockhead ever wrote for money." (Perhaps Johnson, a passionate poet as well as a successful dictionary editor, was being ironic in suggesting otherwise.) Ultimately, the financial prospects for writers in Icelandic are not that different from those of most writers in English. Iceland simply lacks the wildly unrepresentative example of J. K. Rowling to delude anyone.

Motivating Authors

Many scholars speak of copyright protection as solving a "public good" problem. Books are a public good because they have social value, and because it is difficult to prevent people from sharing in them without paying. Copyright protection turns literary works into a more conventional "private good," which individuals must pay to access. Only in this way, the dominant theory goes, can we ensure that authors go on writing. The unstated assumption is that authors write in order to get paid. Yet empirical research reveals that motivations other than money are far more powerful.

A parallel exists between writing books and playing sports. A tiny fraction of athletes—the very best of the best—become professionals. These elite few earn enough to focus full-time on honing their athletic talents. In a handful of cases, they earn enough to inspire significant envy. Yet surely no one would subscribe to the statement, "No one but a blockhead ever played sports, except for money." We easily recognize athletic endeavor as intrinsically rewarding. It challenges us, it is fun, it connects us to other people and, when done well, it brings a sense of accomplishment. While high-earning professional athletes surely enjoy their wealth, we tend to believe that even they play mostly "for the love of the game." So it is also with writing. It is worthwhile to enable the most talented few to dedicate themselves full-time to stretching the boundaries of their craft. But in our adulation of professional genius, we should not lose sight of the importance of amateur creativity.

Rather than focus narrowly on creating financial incentives for potential authors, we should think much more broadly about motivating them. Efforts to address book hunger should be intentional about how they appeal to alternative motivations. Pratham Books founder Rohini Nilekani is particularly eloquent on this subject. "If you scratch an author deeply enough, the author wants to be read," she argues. "Especially children's authors. They get it." The most powerful incentive for people to write, illustrate, and translate for Pratham Books is the exciting prospect of reaching hundreds of thousands of children. Equally powerful, Nilekani believes, is a sense of taking part in an important social mission, which she intentionally placed at the heart of the organization. "A lot is possible if you have a societal mission," Nilekani says. "Creating a community around the cause of reading, books, children—this is absolutely critical to the model."

Human beings want more than the material necessities and luxuries of life (though most of us want those too.) We also crave meaning. Creative expression, service to others, and being part of something larger than yourself are prime ways that people seek to make meaning in their lives. Authorship and artistic creativity have long been seen as a form of spiritual expression in a wide variety of cultures. In the European view, copyright protection is justified not primarily as a financial incentive, but as a way to protect and honor the dignity of the author, who has invested his or her personality in the creation. For this reason, it is essential to give appropriate credit to the individuals who helped create a book.

People want to write. What holds most of them back is the difficulty of doing so. There are many more blogs than books because a blog is much easier to execute. Perhaps it is the case that very high financial incentives would motivate more people to overcome the difficulties of writing a book. Even in the most lucrative publishing markets, however, significant financial rewards are rare and cold comfort in the face of writer's block. In niche publishing markets, the elusive prospect of slim royalties simply cannot do this work. A much bigger impact is likely to come from appealing to intrinsic motivations, and from lowering the barriers to writing and publishing books, including barriers related to copyright law. Potential authors in Iceland know it will be easy to find an editor, get published, and have one's book marketed to the entire country. Potential translators of existing works into neglected languages should be given similar confidence.

TWELVE

All Children Reading

In 2015, United Nations delegates set an ambitious goal: by 2030, all children should enjoy a quality primary and secondary education leading to effective learning. To achieve this goal, however, the early reading materials necessary to support literacy development must be in place. The expert consensus is that children should learn to read in their mother tongue; they must understand spoken language before they can learn to read. SIL International tracks more than 7,000 living languages, of which more than 564 are currently in use in primary education. Unfortunately, early literacy materials are inadequate or absent in most of these languages. This creates a situation of extreme book hunger for approximately one billion children.

How many new titles are needed to fill this gap? Children might do with as few as fifty books in their first year of reading. As they begin to develop fluency, however, many more titles are needed. By my estimate, a thousand picture books in each language is an appropriate target for a minimally adequate supply of children's literature to achieve reading fluency. (This is also Room to Read's target figure for stocking a school library.) Approximately 500 neglected languages are currently used in primary education, which generates a total of more than 500,000 new titles needed. Existing efforts by nonprofit publishers have so far created several hundred quality picture books. Perhaps half of these were openly licensed, resulting in several thousand additional translations; less than 1 percent of the need. Clearly, a dramatically more efficient approach to title development is needed.

This chapter sketches out a vision for how existing actors and new partners can meet the global need for multilingual children's literature within a decade. This strategy begins with mass translation of existing children's books, enabled by one or more of the copyright solutions detailed in the previous chapters: permissions, fair use, exceptions, and open licensing. Once the titles are translated, a second challenge remains: expanding distribution strategies so that a billion children can get their hands on these books. Here, it will be essential to take full advantage of both digital and print formats, through both nonprofit and commercial distribution venues.

Mass Translation

To reach global scale, nonprofit publishing must fully leverage existing resources. There is no shortage of gorgeously illustrated children's titles. In English alone, more than 50,000 picture books are in print. Not all of these titles are culturally appropriate for use in developing countries, but a minority are—well more than the one thousand needed for an adequate children's literature. The problem is simply that these are being published in too few languages. Translation is the most direct, cost-effective, and rapid solution to this problem.

Although automatic machine translation is now very advanced for a few languages, translations into neglected languages still rely on human labor. Pratham Books reports paying around fifty dollars per translation through a partnership with Translators Without Borders. At this low rate, 500,000 paid translations would cost around $25 million. Additional strategies can lower this cost even further. A single translation can be adapted to serve one or more lower reading levels much more easily than translating a new story from scratch. Once a 1,500-word story is translated, a 750-word and a 250-word version can be created easily by simplifying the text. Additionally, a good starting point would be to translate into just one hundred languages; this would be sufficient to serve 80 percent of all children. Local volunteers could continue the work of translating books from any of the initial one hundred languages into the lesser-spoken ones. Combining these techniques would reduce the cost to under $1.5 million.

Moving past the first hundred languages to smaller and smaller language communities, it becomes less and less practical to pay for translations, even on a discounted basis. Crowdsourced translation can pick up where paid translation leaves off. Pratham Books, African Storybook Project, and SIL International have all developed online platforms to help ordinary community members translate storybooks. Because user-friendly software already exists, the true challenge is mobilizing enough people to use it. Language development organizations and teacher education programs might provide the necessary infrastructure to develop a critical mass of amateur translators. Facebook might also provide an effective means of targeting users in specific language communities to recruit them as online volunteer translators.

Selection Criteria

Most American stories are not ideal for global use, but a minority are. Stories starring animal characters, both traditional tales such as *Aesop's Fables* and modern ones like *The Gruffalo*, work in any region of the world. Science and nature titles also travel well. The visually spectacular animals in *What Do You Do with a Tail Like That?* by Steve Jenkins need not be locally familiar in order to delight a child. Culturally specific titles can also work globally, and serve to represent the world's diversity. *Imani's Moon, Manjhi Moves a Mountain,* and *Drum Dream Girl* are set in Kenya, India, and Cuba, respectively; but all are easy for any child to relate to. Folk tales such as Tomi dePaola's *Strega Nona* and *The Legend of the Blue Bonnet* also travel well.

I conducted a sampling of English-language picture books to see what percentage of existing titles might be appropriate for global use. I focused on the four categories of books most likely to travel well: science and nature titles, animal stories, folk tales, and multicultural books. Within each category, I sampled one hundred titles to see how many met the following selection criteria for mass translation: 1) an engaging story or concept, 2) high-quality illustrations, and 3) the illustrated characters and settings are not specific to an affluent, white, or Western demographic. My survey confirmed that at least 7,000 good candidates for mass translation exist: more than 500 folk tales, 750 multicultural titles, 1,000 science and nature titles, and more than 5,000 stories featuring animal characters. This is far more than the number needed.

Even a few hundred stories, adapted to different reading levels, could serve as the backbone of a global children's literature for billions of readers. Given this, quality standards should be particularly high. The effort should prioritize delightful titles with gorgeous illustrations. Children should be excited to read these stories over and over. Attention should also be paid to the ethical messages they communicate. In all cultures, stories are used to cultivate ethical values in the next generation. Kindness, generosity, bravery, hard work, studiousness, and service to others are virtues valued in all cultures. The United Nations' Sustainable Development Goals also specifically call for education to promote nonviolence, gender equality, global citizenship, sustainable lifestyles, human rights, and respect for cultural diversity. A new global canon of children's literature should subtly promote these international values.

Clearing Rights for Translation

Commercial publishers have repeatedly demonstrated their willingness to grant free permissions for nonprofit purposes. Unfortunately, it is incredibly inefficient for publishers to award charitable licenses on a one-off basis. As detailed in the previous chapters, this problem has been overcome in other contexts through reliance on blanket permissions, fair use, specific copyright exceptions, and Creative Commons licenses.

The simplest approach would be for publishers to donate translation rights in a coordinated way. In a single contract, a commercial publisher could authorize translations for a dozen or a hundred books into thousands of neglected languages. The global need for source material could be met with as few as 250 titles. Each one could then be adapted into multiple reading levels to meet the goal of 1,000 translated titles per language. Obtaining rights to at least 500 titles would be desirable to ensure greater variety and options. Even at this higher level, any of the Big Five trade publishers could meet the global need single-handedly.

Through the permissions approach, publishers would provide the digital book files, eliminating the need for scanning and software manipulation to remove text from the images. Publishers could also contribute expertise and visibility to advance the project. If publishers are slow to grant permissions for whatever reason, the effort can fall back on fair use, though this entails legal risks that must be carefully managed. New copyright exceptions would provide the strongest basis for efficiently clearing rights. A fourth alternative is for foundations to commission new titles, or purchase rights to existing ones, and place them on Creative Commons licenses. It is not strictly necessary to choose between these four strategies; all can be pursued in tandem.

Funding Translation

One way to fund translation efforts is through foundation grants. Another is to shift resources currently spent developing early-grade textbooks. Although storybooks and textbooks are complementary, the dominant approach has been for national governments and international aid agencies to invest funds in textbook development, to the neglect of storybooks. The problem is that students with access to textbooks but not storybooks rarely become proficient readers.

It is quite possible, however, to teach reading without a textbook. In this approach, each student chooses a story from which to practice reading. The teacher provides group instruction in letter recognition, phonics, and other decoding strategies. The students practice reading for pleasure every day, either individually or in pairs. The storybook approach to reading instruction has several pedagogical advantages. Ample research shows that students' motivation to read is higher when they are able to choose the book themselves. Picture books also allow students to select a book at a "just right" level of difficulty and to learn at their own pace. In contrast, students practicing reading from a textbook that is either too advanced or too basic for their individual skill level are not actually improving. For these reasons, many educators consider the storybook-focused approach to reading instruction superior to the traditional textbook method.

A storybook approach to teaching reading would also help address the unique challenges of multilingual classrooms. A typical teacher in urban Nairobi will have students whose families speak Swahili, Kikuya, Luhya, and Luo. Educators there will teach from an English or Swahili textbook, verbally translating into the other languages as best they can. With the storybook approach, however, the children can each read in their own language. Students can be paired or grouped by the language of choice to take turns practicing reading to each other. Common instruction would still be given in phonics and other decoding strategies applicable in any language. If the same title is available in multiple languages and levels, teachers can also lead shared activities related to the book's themes while each child reads the edition best suited to them.

From Development to Distribution

After translation, the hard work of distribution begins. Perhaps the best precedent for such an immense effort would be universal vaccination campaigns. Several differences, however, make books even more challenging to distribute. Whereas the same vaccine works for every child, half a million different titles must be made available, with the right book, in the right language, going to the right child. Additionally, each child needs to be vaccinated only once or twice in a lifetime, but children need regular access to books for many years. Once a coordinated vaccination campaign is completed, the disease is eradicated and efforts can cease. Printed books, however, fall apart and must continually be replaced.

Digital distribution is critical to overcoming these challenges. Half a million options can be stored in the cloud, to be conveniently searched and accessed anywhere in the world. Every family with a smartphone can possess an extensive home library. Digital books also do not fall apart and never need to be replaced. For these reasons, digital distribution is a necessary part of any strategy that hopes to someday declare book hunger to be eradicated—necessary, but not sufficient. Like any business intent on promoting higher consumption of its goods, we must seek to distribute in as many formats as possible, through as many channels as possible. Print distribution is also essential, and commercial distribution strategies can serve as a powerful complement to non-profit ones.

Digital Strategies

Not every family in the world has a smartphone and a data plan, but nearly every teacher does. Leveraging these existing resources is a cost-effective way to reach most school-age children. Even in very poor countries, school technology resources often permit children to read digital books from phones, tablets, or a projector. Teachers can also distribute book files for children to read at home on the family phone.

Digital distribution does not necessarily require a data plan or even Internet access. In India, some Pratham Books users copy book files onto mobile phone memory cards costing less than a dollar, using these to transfer stories from one phone to another, either locally or across long distances. Mobile memory cards can also be distributed at education conferences, alongside textbook distribution, in marketplaces and on street corners. As digital devices continue to become more powerful and less expensive, the capabilities of digital distribution will further increase.

Several digital library software platforms appropriate for use in developing countries already exist. Nabu.org, formerly known as Library for All, runs one of the best. Pratham Books, African Storybook Project, and the Global Book Alliance also offer attractive digital libraries focused on openly licensed stories. Worldreader currently serves more than a million readers in developing countries through its mobile app, and is capable of scaling to serve many times more.

The primary factor limiting digital distribution is neither hardware nor software, but awareness. However wonderful a resource, people cannot use it if they do not know it exists. National and state education departments will be an essential partner in making sure teachers know where to access free digital books. Developing-country governments routinely run public awareness campaigns through posters and radio, which could emphasize reading and explain how to access content. Facebook could be particularly effective for spreading multilingual storybooks, because its users are networked with others who speak the same language. Given the high demand for multilingual content, cell phone companies might also be interested enough to preinstall a reading app and zero-rate storybook downloads as a selling point. Every printed copy of a book can also serve as an advertisement for the online resources.

Print Strategies

Print strategies are no less important than digital ones. The primary way that less-well-off children access books in the United States is through their classrooms and school libraries. This will also be essential to reaching children in developing countries. In some countries, textbook distribution is highly efficient; printed storybooks could be distributed in the same way. In other countries, textbooks too often go missing as a result of corruption and theft. Either way, it would be a mistake to rely on schools as the only distribution route.

Getting print books into children's homes should be a top priority. Extensive research shows that book ownership has a powerful impact on reading, educational achievement, and future income. Imagination Library is already working on adapting its direct-to-home distribution model for countries without reliable postal systems. In Belize, the organization sends a shipping container of books every three months, then distributes the copies monthly through churches. Another approach to targeting vulnerable households could be to incorporate book distribution and shared reading into home visits by community health workers.

A variety of print formats should be used. Nonprofit publishers generally favor paperback binding, which is cheaper both to print and to ship on a per-copy basis. Hardcover printing may be more economical in the long run, however, and should not be ruled out without a careful cost-benefit analysis. An even more durable material is the polyethylene fabric popularized by Indestructibles books. Their light weight and slim profile allow them to ship as cheaply as paperbacks, but they are even more durable than hardcover books. Yet another approach is to distribute storybooks on magazine paper, inside newspapers of the same language. Such fragile books would not survive much handling, but they would be incredibly cheap to print and distribute.

The primary challenge of print distribution is the complexity of supplying so many different versions in highly multilingual environments. The best solution to this problem lies in the strategy of mass customization. This approach waits until the last step in a supply chain to customize the product for each consumer. For example, wine bottles are sold in very few sizes and styles. Only once each batch of wine is prepared does a vineyard customize its bottles with a label unique to each wine. Apple's global smartphone distribution system provides a second example. Consumers can choose a variety of memory capacities and case colors, but each phone is fully assembled only once a particular order is paid for. Customizing products at the last step in the supply chain avoids the need to stockpile all possible combinations.

Similarly, a book distributor could warehouse two hundred titles with no text printed on the pages. Once a certain title, in a certain language, at a certain reading level is ordered, clear adhesive labels could be printed with the appropriate text. These labels could be affixed to each page by local employees with the relevant language skills. Alternatively, a school or library might take delivery of empty books with blank sticker sheets, to do their own printing and attaching. Through a global canon approach, the benefits of mass customization could extend worldwide. A limited selection of titles would be produced in huge quantities, allowing for economies of scale in printing and shipping. A few hundred titles could be customized into millions of unique versions to serve every language and level.

Cost Recovery

Digital books can be shared for free, but when it comes to print distribution, cost-recovery strategies are key. No nonprofit raises enough money to give away billions of books as hard copies. To fund such extensive production and distribution efforts, it will be essential to leverage the ability and willingness of many families, schools, and nonprofits to purchase books, when the prices are set as low as possible. First Book has had great success with this model in the United States. In some countries, however, the law prohibits nonprofit organizations from selling goods.

An easier approach might be to eliminate taxes on sales of books in neglected languages. This would avoid the need for small mission-driven publishers and book dealers to legally organize as not-for-profit charities. If profit is not prohibited, additional methods of sustainable print distribution may emerge. Tiny shops could stock books in local languages. Neighborhood microentrepreneurs could open up book rental services from their home. Churches and other trusted community organizations might collect orders from families where postal delivery would be too expensive, perhaps as an institutional fundraiser. Peddlers might sell books on city sidewalks, in marketplaces, and door-to-door. Countries could still collect tax on commercial trade in books in English, French, and other profitable languages.

Enabling market-based print distribution requires special care for the method of clearing rights. Publishers donating rights in neglected languages should not insist on nonprofit distribution methods only. Many small mission-driven organizations in developing countries organize as for-profit companies, even though they make little or no profit. Authors and nonprofits choosing open licenses to maximize the impact of their titles should avoid terms prohibiting commercial use. Fair use rulings and statutory copyright exceptions should be careful to provide room for low-cost distribution of translated materials. Markets fail miserably at creating mother-tongue reading material, but they excel at inexpensively producing and moving physical goods in an open and competitive environment. This strength should be leveraged.

A Book in Every Hand

Music and cuisine are everywhere the product of cultural exchange and localization. This can become true of children's literature as well. Utilizing a mass translation strategy, we can realistically create an adequate book supply for 95 percent of the world's children within a few years. Time is of the essence—and not just to reach the 2030 goal of all children learning well. A strategy that takes another decade longer will come too late for hundreds of millions of children. The first key to this approach is solving the copyright licensing dilemma. Blanket licensing, fair use, copyright exceptions, and open licensing all hold the potential to unlock existing resources. Once translation is accomplished, digital distribution scales up rapidly and inexpensively. Developing an effective ecosystem for print distribution is likely to require greater time.

In the twentieth century, coordinated partnerships of charity, volunteers, government, and industry successfully eradicated smallpox and polio. Similar partnerships will be critical to the campaign to end book hunger. If we succeed, the effects will be transformative for one billion children now in school and for their communities. My own expertise is in copyright law, but you have other unique skills. To further explore how you can put them to use to advance this important cause, I invite you to visit www.bookhunger.org and to continue the conversation with #bookhunger.

Organizations Profiled

African Storybook Project
Publishes multilingual digital stories
Experiments with digital delivery mechanisms
www.africanstorybook.org

Benetech
Reformats books for readers with disabilities
Advocates internationally for copyright exceptions
www.benetech.org

BookDash
Innovated a "hackathon" model for title development
Creates openly licensed books for South African children
www.bookdash.org

Books for Asia
Ships books donated by U.S. publishers to Asian libraries
Supports community creation of multilingual digital stories
www.asiafoundation.org/what-we-do/books-for-asia

Computerized Books for the Blind and Print Disabled
Introduced digital publishing for blind readers
Later merged into Recording for the Blind, now Learning Ally
www.learningally.org

First Book
Helps teachers and charities obtain low-cost books
Incentivizes publishers to produce diverse books
www.firstbook.org

Imagination Library
Dolly Parton's Imagination Library
Mails free books to children up to five years old
www.imaginationlibrary.com

Library for All/Nabu.org
Offers free e-books to mobile users in developing countries
Runs workshops to produce mother-tongue children's books
www.nabu.org

PJ Library
Delivers free books celebrating Jewish culture
A program of the Harold Grinspoon Foundation
www.pjlibrary.org

Pratham Books
Publishes print and digital stories for Indian children
Created the StoryWeaver platform for open creativity
www.storyweaver.org.in

Room to Read
Sets up school libraries in developing countries
Produces original mother-tongue children's books
www.roomtoread.org

SIL International
Developed the Bloom translation software
Supports mother-tongue publishing
www.sil.org

We Need Diverse Books
Raises awareness of the need for diversity in publishing
Sponsors diverse authors and publishing professionals
www.diversebooks.org

Worldreader
Runs mobile reading programs in Ghana, India, and Kenya
Works to demonstrate the potential of digital reading
www.worldreader.org

Bibliography

Accessible Books Consortium. *Books for All: A Starter Kit for Accessible Publishing in Developing and Least Developed Countries.* http://www.accessiblebooksconsortium.org.

Alidou, H., A. Boly, B. Brock-utne, Y. S. Diallo, K. Heugh, and H. E. Wolf, eds. *Optimizing Learning and Education in Africa—The Language Factor: A Stock-Taking Research on Mother Tongue and Bilingual Education in Sub-Saharan Africa.* Paris, France: Association for the Development of Education in Africa, 2006.

Allington, Richard L. "What I've Learned About Effective Reading Instruction from a Decade of Studying Exemplary Elementary Classroom Teachers." *The Phi Delta Kappan* 83, No. 10 (June 2002): 740–747.

Allington, Richard L., Anne McGill-Franzen, Gregory Camilli, Lunetta Williams, Jennifer Graff, Jacqueline Zeig, Courtney Zmach, and Rhonda Nowak. "Addressing Summer Reading Setback Among Economically Disadvantaged Elementary Students." *Reading Psychology* 31, no. 5 (2010).

Association for the Development of Education in Africa. *Formulating Education Policy: Lessons and Experiences from Sub-Saharan Africa.* Oct. 18–22, 1995.

Beebe, Barton. "An Empirical Study of U.S. Copyright Fair Use
Opinions, 1978–2005." University of Pennsylvania Law Review
156 (2008): 549.

Benkler, Yochai. *The Wealth of Networks: How Social Production
Transforms Markets and Freedom.* New Haven: Yale University
Press, 2003.

Benson, Carol. "Do We Expect Too Much of Bilingual Teachers?
Bilingual Teaching in Developing Countries." *International
Journal of Bilingual Education and Bilingualism*, 7:2–3, 204–221.

Bently, Lionel. "Copyright, Translations, and Relations Between
Britain and India in the Nineteenth and Early Twentieth
Centuries." *Chicago Kent Law Review* 82 (2007): 1181.

Bort, Julie. "Highly Successful YouTube Star and Best-Selling
Novelist John Green Says He Feels Like 'a Fraud.' " *Business
Insider.* Aug. 14, 2015.

Commeyras, Michelle, and Hellen N. Inyega. "An Integrative
Review of Teaching Reading in Kenyan Primary Schools."
Reading Research Quarterly 42, no. 2 (April–June 2007): 258–281.

Cooper, H., K. Charleton, J. C. Valentine, and L. Muhlenbruck.
"Making the Most of Summer School: A Meta-Analytic and
Narrative Review." *Society for Research in Child Development* 65
(2000).

Cooper, H., B. Nye, K. Charlton, J. Lindsay, and S. Greathouse.
"The Effects of Summer Vacation on Achievement Test Scores: A
Narrative and Meta-Analytic Review." *Review of Educational
Research* 66, no. 3 (1996): 227–268.

Crystal, David. *English as a Global Language.* Cambridge University
Press, 2003.

Creative Commons. The State of the Commons. https://stateof.
creativecommons.org/.

Daftuar, Swati. "High on the Hindi List." *The Hindu.* Dec. 19, 2014.
https://www.thehindu.com/features/metroplus/high-on-the-
hindi-list/article6707965.ece.

Deci, Edward L., Richard Koestner, and Richard M. Ryan. "A Meta-
Analytic Review of Experiments Examining the Effect of Extrinsic
Rewards on Intrinsic Motivation." *Psychological Bulletin* 125, no. 6
(1999): 627–688.

Bibliography

Entwisle, Doris, K. L. Alexander, and L. S. Olson. *Children, Schools, and Inequality*. Boulder, Colo.: Westview Press, 1997.

Evans, M. D. R., Jonathan Kelley, and Joanna Sikora, "Scholarly Culture and Academic Performance in 42 Nations." *Social Forces* 92, no. 4 (1 June 2014): 1573–1605.

Ethnologue. *Languages of the World: Summary by Language Size.* https://www.ethnologue.com/statistics/size.

Federal Interagency Forum on Child and Family Statistics. *America's Children: Key National Indicators of Wellbeing, 2017.* https://www.childstats.gov/americaschildren/eco1.asp.

Gaiman, Neil. "Why Our Future Depends on Libraries." *The Guardian.* Oct. 15, 2013.

Gurdon, Meghan Cox. *The Enchanted Hour: The Miraculous Power of Reading Aloud in the Age of Distraction.* New York: HarperCollins, 2019.

Kulpoo, Dhurumbeer. "The Quality of Education: Some Policy Suggestions Based on a Survey of Schools—Mauritius." SACMEQ Policy Research: Report No. 1. Paris: International Institute for Educational Planning, 1998.

Krashen, Stephen, and Fay Shin. "Summer Reading and the Potential Contribution of the Public Library to Improving Reading for Children of Poverty." *Public Library Quarterly* 23 (July 2004): 99–109.

Lemos, Ronaldo. "From Legal Commons to Social Commons: Brazil and the Cultural Industry in the 21st Century." University of Oxford Centre for Brazilian Studies, Working Paper CBS 80-07 13, 2007.

Lindsay, Jim. *Children's Access to Print Material and Education-Related Outcomes: Findings from a Meta-Analytic Review.* Naperville, Ill.: Learning Point Associates, 2010.

Lobachev, Sergey. "Top Languages in Global Information Production, Partnership." *The Canadian Journal of Library and Information Practice and Research* 3, no. 2 (2008).

McGill-Franzen, Anne, and Richard Allington, "What Are They to Read?" *Education Week.* October 13, 1993.

McGill-Franzen, et al. "Putting Books in the Classroom Seems Necessary But Not Sufficient." *The Journal of Educational Research* 93 (Nov.–Dec. 1999): 67–74.

McQuillan, Jeff, and Julie Au. "The Effect of Print Access on Reading Frequency." *Reading Psychology* 22 (2001): 225–248.

Neil Butcher and Associates. "The Impact of Open Licensing on the Early Reader Ecosystem." 2016. https://files.eric.ed.gov/fulltext /ED568401.pdf.

Neuman, S. B., and D. Celano. "Access to Print in Low-Income and Middle-Income Communities: An Ecological Study of Four Neighborhoods." *Reading Research Quarterly.* November 2001.

Neuman, S. B., and D. Celano. *Giving Our Children a Fighting Chance: Affluence, Literacy, and the Development of Information Capital.* New York: Teachers College Press, 2012.

Neuman, Susan B., and Naomi Moland. "Book Deserts: The Consequences of Income Segregation in Children's Access to Print." *Urban Education.* 2016. DOI: 10.1177/0042085916654525.

Neuman, Susan. "Books Make a Difference: A Study of Access to Literacy." *Reading Research Quarterly.* July/Aug./Sept. 1999.

Nimmer, David. " 'Fairest of Them All' and Other Fairy Tales of Fair Use." *Law and Contemporary Problems* 66 (2003): 263.

Nussbaum, Martha. "Creating Capabilities: The Human Development Approach." 2011. https://www3.nd.edu/~ndlaw /prog-human-rights/london-symposium/CreatingCapabilities.pdf.

Okediji, Ruth, ed. *Copyright Law in an Age of Limitations and Exceptions.* Cambridge University Press, 2017.

Olian, Irwin. "International Copyright and the Needs of Developing Countries: The Awakening at Stockholm and Paris." *Cornell International Law Journal* 7 (1974): 81.

Piwowar, Heather, et al. "The State of OA: A Large-Scale Analysis of the Prevalence and Impact of Open Access Articles." *PeerJ*, March 2018. https://peerj.com/articles/4375/.

Read Aloud 15 Minutes. *Survey Report: How America Reads Aloud to Its Children.* 2018. http://www.readaloud.org/documents/ ReadAloudSurveyReport.pdf.

Ronen, Shahar, et al. "Links that speak: the global language network and its association with global fame." *Proceedings of the National Academy of Sciences,* 2014. https://doi.org/10.1073/ pnas.1410931111.

Samuelson, Pamela. "Unbundling Fair Uses." *Fordham Law Review* 77 (2007–2008): 2537.

Silbey, Jessica. *The Eureka Myth: Creators, Innovators, and Everyday Intellectual Property.* Stanford University Press, 2014.

SIL International. *Ethnologue: Languages of the World.* 2018, online edition. https://www.ethnologue.com/.

Smith, Keith. "Books and Development in Africa—Access and Role." *Library Trends,* Spring 1978, 469.

Southern and Eastern African Consortium for Monitoring Educational Quality, SACMEQ Policy Issues Series, No.6, September 2010.

United Nations Educational, Scientific, and Cultural Organisation (UNESCO). *Reading in the Mobile Era: A Study of Mobile Reading in Developing Countries.* United Nations, 2014.

United Nations Educational, Scientific, and Cultural Organisation (UNESCO). "Every Child Should Have a Textbook." *Global Education Monitoring Report,* Policy Paper 23, January 2016.

United States Agency for International Development (USAID). *Landscape Report on Early Grade Literacy.* August 6, 2016.

United States Agency for International Development (USAID). *Best Practices for Developing Supplemental Reading Materials.* February 2014.

Vision Loss Expert Group. "Magnitude, Temporal Trends, and Projections of the Global Prevalence of Blindness and Distance and Near Vision Impairment: A Systematic Review and Meta-Analysis." *Lancet Global Health* 5 (2017): 888–897.

Waldfogel, Joel. *The Tyranny of the Market: Why You Can't Always Get What You Want.* Cambridge: Harvard University Press, 2007.

Whitehead, Nicole. "The Effects of Increased Access to Books on Student Reading Using the Public Library." *Reading Improvement* 41 (Fall 2004): 165.

Acknowledgments

At the earliest stages of this research project, I struggled terribly with what questions I ought to ask, and what themes I should focus on. Chris Sprigman, a copyright colleague at NYU, helpfully advised me to "Just start talking to people." After a dozen interviews, he assured me, you'll have some hunches, and another dozen interviews will refine them. With his encouragement, I took the leap of faith and began to reach out to people. They in turn took their own leap of faith that my project would end up being worth their time. I am grateful for their generosity with their time, their expertise, and the individual insights they shared toward this common whole. A few leaders in the nonprofit publishing and copyright spaces, who are not quoted within the book, contributed particularly important insights. Penelope Bender, T. J. Bliss, Colleen Chien, Cable Green, Gautam John, Micah May, Lily Nyariki, Dana Schmidt, and Paul Stacey all deserve personal mention.

I owe a special intellectual debt to my former professors, Jack Balkin and Yochai Benkler. While I was still a law student, they helped connect my interests in human rights and economic development with intellectual property law through the lens of "access to knowledge." Jack went on to play an outsized role in my development as a scholar, sponsoring my fellowship at the Yale Information Society Project for three years, before I took my first tenure-track position. As for Yochai, his scholarship on nonmarket production of information goods was foundational to this work. Other particularly important scholarly influences on my approach to the study of copyright law from the perspective of distributive justice include: Keith Aoiki, James Boyle, Margaret Chon, Julie Cohen, Laurence Helfer, Amy Kapsczynski, Ronaldo Lemos, Molly Land, Chidi Oguamanam, Ruth Okediji, Jerome Reichman, Nagla Rizk, Madhavi Sunder, and Peter Yu.

My colleagues at Indiana University McKinney School of Law were unfailingly supportive. Susan DeMaine, Yvonne Dutton, Frank Emmert, Ben Keele, Florence Roisman,

Margaret Ryznar, Carlton Waterhouse, and George Wright deserve particular acknowledgment for their feedback and assistance with this work. So does Chinese copyright scholar Xiaohao Zhang, whom we were very lucky to host from the School of Economics and Finance at Xi'an International Studies University. Special thanks are also due to the students in my Copyright, Human Rights, and Intellectual Property courses who shared helpful feedback and contributed valuable ideas as this project evolved. I want to personally thank several students who contributed significantly to this project, most now accomplished lawyers in their own right: Alyssa Devine, Jessica Dickinson, Nicole Dobias, Clark Giles, Kayla Hill, Annalee Patel, and Anne Young.

Colleagues beyond my own school or field also generously shared their time, advice, and thoughts to make this book a reality. Mark McKenna shared valuable comments at the earliest presentation of this research at Yale Law School's Innovation Without IP conference. Numerous colleagues offered other helpful input at UC Santa Clara, the Kent-DePaul Intellectual Property Colloquium, the IP Scholars Conference, and Indiana University Maurer School of Law's workshop for junior legal scholars. Erin Delaney was the first to push me to see this book as one that large numbers of "real people" might want to read. Mark Tushnet helped me translate that vague hope into the right language for my book proposal. Joseph Singer is responsible for convincing me to take the metaphor of "book hunger" as the book's central focus. (I had originally conceived the title as *Social Publishing: Ending Book Hunger Through Mission-Driven Innovation*.) Fortunately Anupam Chander had introduced me to my editor on this book, Joseph Calamia, who believed in the academic/ trade crossover potential of this project even with the original title. I am particularly grateful to Joe and to Yale University Press for ensuring this work could be published on a Creative Commons license.

Because this book was imagined for a mixed audience, I also drew heavily upon the kindness of family and friends as readers. Sarah Green brought an art docent's perspective to an early draft of the proposal and pushed me to reconceive the framing to make the narrative more readable. Romana Solovan and Oluwatobilola Kappo each read multiple chapters to flag words and phrases that would be problematic for readers who are not native English speakers. A veritable fleet of taxi, Uber, and Lyft drivers served as thought partners over the years, sharing their own personal experiences with access to books in contexts as diverse as Indiana, Bangladesh, and Ethiopia, and helping me to find the right words to describe this project. My parents-in-law, Mike and Jan Shaver, welcomed discussion of these ideas around their dinner table, and my father-in-law read many draft chapters.

I feel a special personal debt to the family members who were most directly responsible for my own passion for books. My mother, Lucia D'Andrea Bishop, was a kindergarten teacher. She made sure that I enjoyed a steady diet of books throughout my childhood, from libraries and garage sales. Among the many humanitarian and community roles her father filled in his life, Joseph D'Andrea served on the board of the local public library in Spangler, Pennsylvania. Although the town was so small its library no longer exists, my grandfather's position of authority impressed me enormously as a young child, and made our many shared trips to the tiny Spangler library all the more magical. My granny Marjorie McGee D'Andrea, my father Kelley Bishop, his parents, and numerous aunts and uncles were also important models of avid reading as I grew up. Today it is my joy to share books with my own daughters: Josephine (9), Eleanor (6), and Margot (3).

Finally and most importantly, I struggle to find the words that can do justice to the impact that my husband had on this project. I have often noticed acknowledgments in which the authors thank their spouses for their patience. Now I understand why. Such a large undertaking requires sacrifices of time and energy from both the writer and the ones closest to them. Bob Shaver is not only my life partner and co-parent, but also my most important thought partner. We must have spent a hundred hours in conversation about my most recent thoughts and findings. His comments and questions, drawing upon his professional experience in nonprofit strategic consulting, always helped to generate new insights. Thank you, Bob. Your partnership makes me a better person.

Index

Index

Index

Index

Index